Celebrate Your Freedom

"If the Son sets you free, you are truly free."

John 8:36

Inspiring Stories and Messages from Come to the Fire

Edited by Patsy Lewis

Celebrate Your Freedom

"If the Son sets you free, you are truly free."

John 8:36

Inspiring Stories and Messages

from

Come to the Fire

Copyright © 2016 Come to the Fire Publishing
Published by Come to the Fire Publishing
PO Box 480052
Kansas City, MO 64148
cometothefire.org
Library of Congress Cataloging in Publication Data:
ISBN 978-0-9905903-5-4
Printed in the United States of America

Table of Contents

5

Preface

Patsy Lewis[1]

The book you hold in your hand is a compilation of Come to the Fire stories and messages celebrating the freedom that comes in knowing Jesus and giving Him "all of me for all of Him."

Jesus boldly proclaimed, "I am the way, the truth, and the life. No one can come to the Father except through me" (John 14:6). Jesus said to those who believed in Him, "You are truly my disciples if you remain faithful to my teachings. And you will know the truth, and the truth will set you free" (John 8:31-32).

Christ within gives freedom to:
- Come to the Fire
- Behold His Glory
- Discover Your Promise
- Receive Your inheritance
- Reflect His Glory
- Enter His Rest
- Overflow with Love
- Embrace the Cross

This results in a celebration of freedom that has many facets and is available to all who accept God's invitation to come to the fire and be cleansed of sin, purified and made whole, consumed by His amazing grace, and overcome by His unfailing love.

The stories within these pages give witness that when "the Son sets you free, you will be free indeed" (John 8:36 NIV).

The Come to the Fire Vision

Aletha Hinthorn

The desire for a conference that calls women to love God with all their hearts had been in my heart for over a decade. When Beth Coppedge, a lady I had met at a retreat in Ohio, called me in 2002, I had no idea God was summoning us to pray for such an event. "Would you like to join with a few of us to pray at an Amish Inn in Ohio?" she asked. I loved the idea, and for several years, a few of us met nearly every six months for three days to seek God.

We shared the burden for God to revive the message of scriptural holiness in our land—the message that God purifies our hearts so we can live holy lives by the power of the Holy Spirit. God's consuming fire can set us free from self so we find it possible to say with Jesus, "I seek not to please myself but him who sent me" (John 5:30 NIV). This is the gracious promise we wanted to proclaim.

In the spring of 2004, Charme Fletcher, a pastor's wife, emailed me about the need for a deeper life conference for women. Four of us met that summer, discussed it, and committed to pray and ask others to pray. In October a friend, not knowing of Charme's emails and our prayers, wrote she was sensing that "the Lord is prompting us to move forward on the women's conference we've had the vision for." After two days of emails, this friend wrote, "Okay, Aletha! The ball's in your court....The main thing I sense is that we just get the ball rolling!" When I read that, it seemed that indeed I caught the ball. The "ball" came as a desire to bring together a few women who would share the vision of calling women to an intimate walk with Jesus.

How was I to begin planning such a conference? In 1998, a woman said God gave her Joshua 3:3-4 for me: "When you see the ark of the covenant of the LORD your God, and the Levitical priests carrying it, you are to move out from your positions and follow it. Then you will know which way to go, since you have never been this way before" (NIV). I now understood that these words applied to this new challenge. It was true, I had not gone this way before, so I knew I must follow the "Ark"—the precious Holy Spirit within. With each decision, I must know what the Spirit wanted.

In January 2005, nine women from six states met in my home for three days to pray and discuss a women's conference. We had no interest in just another conference, but we sensed a need to give women the distinctive message that love for Jesus can be the controlling passion in our lives. This truth burned within us as the message of hope we had to give. Jesus saves—He saves us from our need to be controlled by self-interests. We can, indeed, love God with all our hearts. We wanted to promote the message that God not only cleanses our hearts and inner desires and motives, but that we can live fully satisfied and victorious in Jesus no matter our circumstances. Thus, we crafted a mission statement with vision objectives and began to move forward.

The night before the women arrived, I told my pastor, Dr. J. K. Warrick, of this vision. He immediately responded, "You can have this at College Church." Because of this invitation, the first three conferences were at College Church of the Nazarene in Olathe, Kansas. Since then we've been in Nashville, Tennessee; Ft. Wayne, Indiana; Bourbonnais, Illinois; Holland, Michigan; and twice in Grove City, Ohio.

Matthew Henry said, "When God intends great mercy for His people, He first of all sets them to praying." God not only put this conference on the hearts of many individuals and prayer groups, but He chose and equipped Patsy Lewis to be our prayer coordinator. She has gathered many women in the United States and beyond to pray regularly for Come to the Fire. God also sent Nancy Jesudass, a Spirit-called intercessor, to pray for revival to come through Come to the Fire.

God's holy presence came to that first gathering and has descended in each of the conferences since. Many women testify of the deep work God has done in their hearts. One attendee wrote, "Come to the Fire was an outstanding conference, but more than that, it was a holy event. Women from around the world responded with a spontaneous spirit of obedience every time the altar was opened. It was not simply revival of the mind whereby women decide to turn over a new leaf, but it was revival of the heart that changed our lives forever."

We soon realized that God had more in mind than just a conference. Beth suggested we form Lydia Prayer Groups around the world to unite in prayer for revival. Patsy coordinates Lydia Prayer, and a massive network of praying groups of women, teens, and children has emerged. Twelve Lydia Prayer Retreats have been held in various states.

Kim McLean, a Dove Award winning songwriter and Come to the Fire council member, leads song-writing retreats for the worship team. Scores of new songs centered on the holiness message have been written with five CDs recorded.

More than a dozen new books have been published bearing the message of the holy heart, and daily devotionals go out Monday through Friday to encourage and challenge thousands of women in their daily walk with Christ.

While we're grateful for the many lives that have been transformed by God through the ministry of Come to the Fire, I long for an even greater outpouring of the Spirit. My heart joins in Jesus' prayer for His Church: "...may they be brought to complete unity. Then the world will know that you sent me..." (John 17:23 NIV).

Ezekiel 47 speaks of a small stream of water coming out from under the threshold of the temple. Then it became ankle deep, then knee deep. Finally it was deep enough to swim in and so wide that it was an uncrossable river. The small stream of water speaks of the outpouring of the Holy Spirit on the Day of Pentecost, but we are not to look back to the Day of Pentecost for the greatest outpouring of the Spirit. Ezekiel's river from the temple teaches us that we can anticipate an even greater visitation of the Spirit than we've had in the past.

Joel 2:23 refers to this outpouring as the latter rain. Then Zechariah wrote, "Ask the LORD for rain in the time of the latter rain" (Zechariah 10:1 NKJV). It is time to ask.

See, I am doing a new thing! Now it springs up; do you not perceive it? I am making a way in the desert and streams in the wasteland (Isaiah 43:19 NIV).

Mission of Come to the Fire

Come to the Fire exists to encourage women to experience the joy of a love relationship with Jesus Christ that expresses itself in holiness of heart and life by the power of the Holy Spirit, and to help them find their place in fulfilling the Great Commission.

Vision of Come to the Fire

Our vision is to bring the holiness message to women around the world. We want to provide conferences and publications that challenge them and equip them to live wholeheartedly for Jesus.

Goals of Come to the Fire

• Encourage scores to pray that women will hunger for holy hearts.

• Publish and distribute materials necessary for women to maintain their commitment to live wholly for Jesus.

• Plan conferences that can be duplicated in other places and in different denominations.

• Use speakers who have the message of loving God with all their hearts as their passion so they can articulate it, not simply as a doctrine, but as the joy and heartbeat of their lives.

• Use musicians who are filled with the Spirit and anointed so that what captivates the women as they sing is not the musician, but the message the Spirit speaks.

• Provide a way for women to receive help after the conferences, such as through books, magazines, CDs, a spiritual life coach, small groups, or emails.

• Provide training for women God would choose to articulate the holiness message in new wineskins.

• Provide new songs that present the beautiful message of surrendering to the lordship of Jesus.

Significance of the Name

The scriptural reason behind calling the conference Come to the Fire came from our first year's theme verse, which was Deuteronomy 5:4. "Moses spoke these words to the Israelites: 'At the mountain the LORD spoke to you face to face from the heart of the fire.'" But Moses reminded them that they were afraid of the fire and did not go.

Why had the Israelites been afraid of the fire? Perhaps they were not ready to stand in His holy presence, but preferred to live by a list of rules. They said to Moses: "Go yourself and listen to what the LORD our God says. Then come and tell us everything He tells you, and we will listen and obey" (Deuteronomy 5:27). So Moses ascended the mountain and brought back the commandments.

Their refusal to go into God's fire had long-term consequences. Within days, they were worshipping the golden calf, and repeatedly, throughout their history, they turned to other idols and failed to obey the law God gave Moses on Mt. Sinai. So God began to speak of a new promise. "I will put my law in their minds and write it on their hearts" (Jeremiah 31:33 NIV). With His law in their hearts, the inclination of their hearts would be turned toward pleasing God rather than pleasing themselves.

God's word in Ezekiel says: "I will give them an undivided heart and put a new spirit in them....Then they will...be careful to keep my laws" (Ezekiel 11:20 NIV). God promises to give us an undivided heart—a heart that has only one motive; that motive is to please Him, and if He is pleased, we are content.

God still invites us to Come to the Fire, and His consuming fire sets us free so we can love Him with all our heart.

16

Part I

Come to the Fire

Aletha Hinthorn

The LORD spoke to you face to face out of the fire on the mountain...."*The LORD our God has shown us his glory and his majesty, and we have heard his voice from the fire*" *(Deuteronomy 5:4, 24 NIV).*

The invitation to the fire is from our Father whose great longing is to draw us close—so He comes as consuming fire. We find that freeing ourselves from pride, misplaced motives, self-centeredness, and unforgiveness to be impossible. We cannot purify our hearts, but His fire can.

"Then suddenly the LORD you are seeking will come to his temple....he will be like a refiner's fire or a launderer's soap. He will sit as a refiner and purifier of silver; he will purify the Levites and refine them like gold and silver" (Malachi 3:1-3 NIV).

Chapter 1

Prayer Paves the Way

Patsy Lewis[1]

Because I love Zion [the Church], I will not keep still. Because my heart yearns for Jerusalem [Zion], I cannot remain silent. I will not stop praying for her until her righteousness shines like the dawn, and her salvation blazes like a burning torch. The nations will see your righteousness. World leaders will be blinded by your glory. And you will be given a new name by the LORD'S own mouth. The LORD will hold you in his hand for all to see—a splendid crown in the hand of God (Isaiah 62:1-3).

In September 2005, I attended a leadership gathering where I received a brochure about a women's conference scheduled in the Kansas City area the next fall. A brief statement regarding Lydia Prayer Groups forming intrigued me. My thoughts immediately dismissed the idea of attending since I already had a full schedule; however, I acquired the director's phone number and left a voicemail with Aletha Hinthorn inquiring about the

Lydia groups. In her message back to me, she said Beth Coppedge was leading that effort.

Since I was living about a hundred miles from Beth, I drove to meet with her a couple of weeks later. She shared her heart about forming small prayer groups around the world based on the story of Lydia in Acts 16. She then turned to me and said, "What do you think?" In less than an hour, she had invited me to be the Lydia Prayer Coordinator and suggested that perhaps I was to be the prayer chaplain for the women's conference being planned for the following October. Besides that, she invited me to go with her and a group of ladies to Budapest, Hungary in January for a European Women's Conference. This was a staggering thought! She then took me to her Titus Women's office and introduced me to Vicki New who was working on a Lydia Prayer Guide. They showed me the work in progress. That was the beginning of my journey with Lydia Prayer, Come to the Fire, and the European Women's Conference on the Holy Heart. As we parted in the parking lot, Beth said, "I can't wait to call Aletha!"

Early the next morning as I sat pondering Beth's request and listening for God's direction, these are the words He spoke to me: "You received a surprise yesterday, didn't you? It is in My plan. You feel humbled and overwhelmed, but I will be your right hand. Your interest in the Lydia groups the first time you read about them came from Me."

When I returned home from Tennessee a couple of days following my first meeting with Beth, I had an email from Aletha with this message: "This morning at breakfast, I told Daniel: 'Patsy is meeting with Beth today. I wonder if she is supposed to be our prayer coordinator. Perhaps I should call Beth.'" Then she continued, "But God went before me."

Come to the Fire was bathed in prayer. I gathered a prayer team from around the nation and beyond. It grew from fifty to seventy-five, then to more than a hundred and continued to multiply as these prayer partners spread my requests to their ministry teams and prayer groups. I discovered new praying "sisters" everywhere I traveled as God gave opportunities to share about Come to the Fire and the Lydia Prayer vision.

Lydia Prayer Groups began to form in many states and several continents—small groups praying for revival and God's glory to be revealed in our personal lives, our families, churches, communities, and the nations of the world. In addition to Lydia Prayer Guides, leaders' materials were prepared. Altar Workers' Packets for Come to the Fire were assembled; prayer leaders were called; and prayer suggestions were sent to those registering to attend the first conference.

As I read my journals from that year, I am flabbergasted at how God carried me those months leading up to Come to the Fire. Just weeks before the conference, my eighty-nine year old mother fell in my home and broke her hip. She was still in a rehabilitation center when I traveled to Olathe, Kansas. I was advised that she would not be able to come home, and I would need to find a care facility for her. This was not the only major crisis I was facing in my family. With a lump in my throat, I felt as if I had been through the fire as I made my way to Come to the Fire. Tuesday morning, October 10, 2006, at 6:30 a.m., before I left home to travel the miles ahead, God gave me this message:

"I am calling you to come to the Fire. In that Fire is purifying and purging, power and illumination. Again, I say to you: Fear not, for I am with you—as you drive, prepare, lead, listen, and speak. Do not become overcome with details. I am your God—not just the God of all the women leaders—giants of faith I am bringing together this week. There will also be many fragile ones who look exceedingly put together on the exterior but are crumbling on the interior. I am their God, too. Point them to Me. Take many opportunities to pray. Lift others into My presence. I will be powerful among you. Expect the unexpected. You live by My power. I am in you and you in Me. I am giving you authority to build up. Extend My touch—My love. My grace and love will go with you."

As God promised, His grace and love did go with me. He met with us as prayer team members and the council came together early to pray and read Scripture on the property where this great event would be held. His presence was near in the altar encouragers' meeting Thursday afternoon. He helped us adapt when the opening night speaker's flight was cancelled, and He gave His servant Beth Coppedge a powerful message to deliver to us in that first service. We had given God the conference from the very beginning and allowed Him to rearrange plans as He chose. Ladies were praying in homes and hotel rooms every hour throughout the night Thursday and Friday. I was awake most of the night Friday praying for the closing sessions Saturday. I received text messages at 3:00 a.m. telling me how one prayer partner was praying for me.

Early Saturday morning before anyone else arrived at the church, Monda Simmons and I made our way to the altar to pray. Soon clusters of women were gathering, giving God thanks for His healing and transforming touch on their lives. Ladies prayed for me before I moved to the platform to speak.

His holy presence continued to fill the "temple" until the closing communion service. He met every hungry heart that came to the Fire longing to be purified and healed. Following the conference, I could not talk about it for weeks and still have no words to describe that holy gathering! He has continued to do His amazing work at each Come to the Fire conference. Perhaps the God stories in this book will give you a tiny glimpse of His powerful work in the lives of women totally in love with Jesus!

I tell you the truth, anyone who has faith in me will do the same works I have done, and even greater works, because I am going to be with the Father. You can ask for anything in my name, and I will do it, so that the Son can bring glory to the Father (John 14:12-13).

Chapter 2

Revival of the Heart

Sharon Bushey[1]

Won't you revive us again, so your people may rejoice in you? Show us your unfailing love, O LORD, and grant us your salvation (Psalm 85:6).

We were women who represented many generations, cultures, races, and walks of life. The majority of us had traveled many miles and had overcome a myriad of hurdles in order to attend. We were women who had "Come to the Fire" wanting to be "pure as gold, but finer than gold."[2] The Fire would refresh, refine, and revive. More than 1200 of us gathered in Olathe, Kansas. Women traveled from thirty-five states, including Alaska and Hawaii. Ladies also represented Canada, the Bahamas, Indonesia, Korea, Uganda, and France. Missionaries came from Asia, Europe, Africa, North America, and South America.

I felt a special move of the Spirit in my own heart as the planning committee and praise team approached the platform for the opening service. This was the appointed

23

time for the revival fire to fall on this group of expectant hearts. In the opening comments, Aletha Hinthorn spoke her faith, "Not only are you here, but also God is here."

As Melinda Priest and the praise team led us in worship, the words of each song had fresh messages for our souls. We wanted the revival fire to fall on this conference so that the "Holy Spirit...would rain down... over our church and over our lives."[3] Some of us sang with enthusiasm while others wiped tears as whispered words of songs were spoken. Yet others could not sing at all as the voices of their hearts were lifted heavenward in prayer. When Kim McLean and Devon O'Day introduced the theme song "Come to the Fire," a holy presence beyond description settled over us. It seemed I could sense the angels en masse hovering among us as God sat on His throne, smiling in approval while His women worshipped Him. The women in this place were going to experience "souls purified, a new day begun."[4]

Since the Holy Spirit tailor-made each message to fit our individual needs, it is difficult to summarize what we learned. Nevertheless, Beth Coppedge's words struck a chord in many of us when she said, "I was so busy working for God that I was not a lover of God." She convinced us that "all God wants is a squeaky clean woman with a squeaky clean heart" who will focus on loving Him, not just working for Him. We also learned that ministry happens in ordinary places. Many of us are waiting for stages on which to perform or pulpits from which to speak, while God is calling us to use our ordinary kitchen tables as places to learn to love Him and share His Word.

Dr. Nina Gunter exhorted us to keep in mind that Christian perfection is not flawless performance, flawless judgment, or flawless communication, but it is perfection of purpose. The experience of being wholly sanctified is not death to self but death of self. When we are wholly sanctified, we submit to continual instruction, and we live with a repentant spirit.

At the close of the Friday evening service, Carolyn Johnson reminded us that forgiveness is often the key to our physical and emotional healing. The sanctuary was filled with weeping as women unloaded their heavy, debilitating burdens of unforgiveness. To the praise of Jesus, hearts, bodies, and relationships were healed in those precious moments of intercessory forgiveness.

It was like the day of Pentecost when people gathered from every nation. We heard not only in our spoken tongue, but also in the language of our individual hearts. Those who had experienced the cleansing and infilling work of the Holy Spirit thanked God the message of holiness was still being preached and lived. Discouraged Christians felt His warm embrace and were encouraged to keep the fire burning. New believers heard the call to grow in faith and experience the fire. The lost heard the call to repentance, and one lady testified to becoming a transformed Rahab.[5]

Throughout this "Holy Event," as my friend Joy called it, we were reminded that holiness is not just an ancient theology but a real way of life for women of this century. It is not just a nice way to live; it is a biblical mandate for each believer. Carla Sunberg's stories of life in Russia reminded us that what looks like sacrifice for coming to the Fire is really an incredible journey. When God burns up the trash of our lives and leads us into the holy life led by the Holy Spirit, what remains is the image of God in us.

Before the final service on Saturday morning, we participated in Lydia Prayer Groups as modeled by Patsy Lewis. This time of prayer prepared us for accepting our mission to spread the fire to the world. In the closing moments, all 1200 women joined hands and held them high as our voices resounded in song, "Take your candle; go light the world."

Create in me a pure heart, O God, and renew a steadfast spirit within me. Do not cast me from your presence or take your Holy Spirit from me. Restore to me the joy of your salvation and grant me a willing spirit, to sustain me (Psalm 51:10-12 NIV).

Changed, Renewed, Surrendered, Free

CTTF Attendees

Changed

When I registered for the Come to the Fire conference, I had no idea what the Lord had in store for me. I had attended many retreats and conferences that always left me feeling "filled up," but I had never been to one that left me completely changed until now. From the very first minute of the conference, the Lord's presence was real. He was there all three days, and He lit a fire in me that I brought home. He was even with me on the bathroom floor of my hotel room at 3:00 a.m. while I was praying as part of the all-night prayer session.

I have known the Lord nearly all my life; sometimes I followed Him more than others, but I had never completely given everything to Him. I have a husband, two very active children, and I work full time. My children and husband are always the victims of my "expectations." Sometimes my expectations have been too much, and my happiness and joy revolved around those expectations. I relied on other people to sustain my fulfillment of life. What a tough life that is! People are only human, and depending on them as a source of fulfillment leads only to disappointment and heartache.

Jesus changed me on Friday, October 13, 2006. Now those days when my children don't mind, Jesus is enough. He is enough when my husband forgets to kiss me good-bye. He is enough when things at work are tough. He is enough when things don't go my way.

While tucking my fourteen-year-old daughter in bed after arriving home from the conference, she said to me, "Mom, you're different."

Yes, thank You, sweet Jesus, I am different![1]

Renewed

I don't think I have ever felt the presence of God as strongly in any other type of meeting or conference as I did at Come to the Fire. I was praying before the conference that God would meet me and give me a fresh sense of Himself. I left knowing He had been faithful to that prayer. Each session was so Christ-centered, and it felt as if Jesus knew He had been invited and was in charge of the time. The message of holiness was presented in an attractive, realistic way that conveyed the message that God is big enough to deliver us from sin.

This conference gave me a renewed belief in the power of prayer. The results of the many hours of prayer for this conference were evident by the atmosphere during each day. Nothing but prayer and dependence on God could have produced the same result.[2]

Surrendered

Beth Coppedge's message Thursday night was like salve to my heart. I knew before she finished speaking that God was dealing with me to surrender to His will in a certain area of my life, and I prayed that she would hurry and finish so I could go pray. The altar of surrender completely set the conference apart from all others.

Dr. Carolyn Johnson's message related to my own journey. I have lived through abuse and totally understand the "intimacy room." My husband and I have been in ministry for nineteen years, and many women in our congregation have been sexually abused and don't know the sweet life that waits on the other side of forgiveness.

Even now, thinking about the weekend brings new tears of total joy from my heart.[3]

Free

I came to the first Come to the Fire for two reasons— to be with a close friend and have a good time. I was expecting to meet people, hear nice music, and have a relaxing get away. I had attended many Christian conferences before, but even though most of them were excellent, convictions and determination to change never lasted long afterwards. So, in my mind, going to Come to the Fire was nothing more than going to another Christian conference. Little did I know! God had an agenda! First, the worship, oh, the worship! I began crying at the first note and did not stop until the end! I felt the presence of Jesus so powerfully in my soul, and I felt lifted up to heaven! Never, never had I worshipped this way before!

When Beth Coppedge shared, she was as funny as she was deep, making the audience alternately laugh and cry. The thought came to mind that it would have been wise to keep this powerful speaker for the end. I pitied the poor woman who was to come after her! Little did I know again! One after the other, all of the ladies were inspirational, knowledgeable, and deeply spirited. Words were spoken that I will never forget—phrases like: "All of you for all of Him!" "Jesus is enough!" "A squeaky clean heart!"

God used the healing service to wrench my heart. As we were going through the motions of repentance and forgiveness, I heard a whisper: "You have not forgiven your ex-husband." God taught me, "You can only forgive when you are not expecting anything from the offender anymore." Searching my heart, it was clear that I was still expecting validation, amends, or recognition from my ex-husband. Since it was not happening, expectations were unfulfilled, anger was lingering underneath, and closure could not take place. In light of this, I had to reconsider all my past relationships. In the process, I realized that I was in the same predicament with my father—still desperately trying to get water from a dry well. It was time to let go, renounce my expectations, and seek validation from my Father in heaven. Then, and only then, was I able to forgive. It was a place of freedom and rest.

Little did I know that Come to the Fire was going to be a life-changing conference bringing healing to areas of my life that I did not even know were damaged![4]

Part II

Behold His Glory

Aletha Hinthorn

For the LORD will rebuild Zion and appear in His glory (Psalm 102:16 NIV).

God will restore His dwelling so He can make us to "be for the display of His splendor" (Isaiah 61:3 NIV). May His Word be fulfilled in you: "I will fill this house with glory" (Haggai 2:7 NIV). We come together to "Behold His Glory."

"I have seen you in the sanctuary and beheld your power and your glory. Because your love is better than life, my lips will glorify you" (Psalm 63:2-3 NIV).

Chapter 3

Living in God's Glory
Linda Boyette

Bring My sons from afar and My daughters from the ends of the earth, everyone who is called by My name, and whom I have created for My glory, Whom I have formed, even whom I have made (Isaiah 43:6-7 NASB). Turn to Me and be saved, all the ends of the earth; For I am God, and there is no other. (Isaiah 45:22 NASB).

I was offered a God-given privilege to speak at Come to the Fire when the theme was "Behold His Glory." Until then I had never taken the time to dive into what the Word of God meant when referring to the term glory. I discovered that every account in Scripture where glory is mentioned, it is in connection with God Almighty. Did you know that whenever individuals, places, or things encounter God's glory, they are never left the same, and when His glory is in the object's midst, it is considered holy?

The Hebrew word for glory is *kabod,* which is defined as weight.[1] This weighty word carries the entire essence and nature of the absolute fullness of God Himself!

The marvel is that the glory of the Almighty God is three persons—Father, Son and Holy Spirit. Notice I didn't say this glory is *in*; this glory *is* three persons! When we speak of God's glory, we are literally speaking of who He is—the I AM, the Absolute Holy One. If man desires to give but one word to define all of God's names, that word well might be glory. Holy Glory! There is absolutely no other god who can claim that within Himself all is! In Him all lives, breathes, and has its existence. He is glory! *He is enough!*

In the first three chapters of Genesis, we find no mention of the terms love, covenant, sanctification, holiness, obedience, sin, or glory. God in His absolute holiness needs no terms. Genesis 1-2 introduces us to our God of glory. He shows man who He is through His works of creation. While many say you can't prove there is a God, "the heavens are telling of the glory of God; and their expanse is declaring the work of His hands. Day to day pours forth speech, and night to night reveals knowledge. There is no speech, nor are there words; their voice is not heard. Their line has gone out through all the earth, and their utterances to the end of the world" (Psalm 19:1-4 NASB). "The heavens proclaim his righteousness, and all peoples have seen His glory" (Psalm 97:6 NASB).

In that garden of Paradise, all creation revealed who He is—absolute selfless, extravagant, holy love. There is no other like God, and there is no other love like God's. God is not a form of love: "God is love" (I John 5:16b). In Paradise absolute selfless, extravagant, holy love is expressed.

At the climax of all His creation, God formed a priceless, precious human being created in the image of God. "Let us create man in Our image, according to Our likeness" (Genesis 1:26 NASB), the image of Father, Son, and Holy Spirit. Man was created to possess this same essence, to reflect the same image as the Triune God. Man only needed to believe and choose God's spoken Word as truth and trust His will to be good. "Let it be...it was so...it was very good!"[2] What was good? His glory! And out of His glory of who He is came the goodness of His creation and His intention for man to be holy as He is holy.

God created man and woman to live the image of God and participate in His glory from the beginning. Adam and Eve were created holy! They were given the Holy Spirit to live free to choose God to be the center and source of all they needed.

The evil one sought to deceive and kill the glory of God. "Look what He is withholding from you. God doesn't mean what He says, His Word is not absolute truth, and He is not absolute love; you can never trust Him."[3] When Eve saw it was attractive, she desired it and ate. If man rejects God's glory for the devil's lie, he exchanges the reality of living for a delusion. Sin always begins when God is not enough.

"For the wrath of God is revealed from heaven against all ungodliness and unrighteousness of men who suppress the truth in unrighteousness, because that which is known about God is evident within them; for God made it evident to them. For since the creation of the world His invisible attributes, His eternal power and divine nature, have been clearly seen, being understood through what has been made, so that they are without excuse. For even though they knew God, they did not honor Him [glorify Him] as God or give thanks....For they exchanged the truth of God for a lie, and worshiped and served the creature rather than the Creator, who is blessed forever. Amen" (Romans 1:18-21, 25 NASB).

After that first sin in the garden, Romans 3:23 describes man's state: "All have sinned and fall short of the glory of God." It doesn't say all have sinned and need forgiven, though we most certainly do. It doesn't say all have sinned and need grace, which we are doomed without. It says we have all sinned and lack His glory. In the old language, glory means presence. God's Word speaks of the iniquity of man. One definition of iniquity is the lack of the presence of holiness. This is the reality; we all have sinned, and turning into our own will and way, we have rejected God's presence—His Glory!

Abraham knew his error; Moses saw his failure; Isaiah saw his center; David recognized his need for a new heart and spirit. There has always been a remnant seeking God and His favor.

The truth of God's intention for His people has never been so articulated as in the Word's written account to Israel. They knew from the very beginning why they were His chosen people; "...you will be my own special treasure from among all the peoples on earth; for all the earth belongs to me...you will be...my holy nation" (Exodus 19:5-6). "Remember that the LORD rescued you from the iron-smelting furnace of Egypt in order to make you his very own people and his special possession, which is what you are today" (Deuteronomy 4:20).

They were invited to know a covenant of lavish love through a sacred fellowship with Father, Son, and Holy Spirit.[4] Chosen to be the habitation of His dwelling, He would be at the very center of living.[5] They were to claim and live in the land of promise with His presence; they would have everything needed for godly living.[6] Through this sacred fellowship with Yahweh, they would reveal the holiness, the glory of God, to every nation and tribe.[7] He was in their midst. "Not one of the good promises which the LORD had made to the house of Israel failed; all came to pass" (Joshua 21:45 NASB).

Only two of the original Israelites arrived into the Promised Land! The sin problem never changes. The children of Israel grumbled, wished for the old life, complained, believed the lie that the way of the pagans looked better than what they had. Oh, they wanted to be His people, but on their terms, in their own way, and through the works of the flesh, so they took matters into their own hands. Instead of knowing God, they sinned against God, and lost the privilege of the reality of God's intention for them. They wanted the blessings of His glory in their midst, but His glory, His presence, was not enough for them. They wanted God plus—God plus their own way, God plus the ways of the world. God Himself was not enough so they built a golden calf. They gave their worship to other gods. "Has a nation changed gods when they were not gods? But My people have changed their glory for that which does not profit" (Jeremiah 2:11 NASB). "I am the Lord, that is My name; I will not give My glory to another, nor my praise to graven images" (Isaiah 42:8 NASB).

God never changes, and His intention for mankind remains the same. God's incessant love longs for man to be His. He had an intervention before the foundation of the world; He Himself would become man and dwell among men.[8] The Son revealed the Father's Glory in every thought, word, and deed; He was God's glory![9] He would fulfill God's will on earth as is done in heaven. His blood, His own life given, would prepare His people to carry His glory. In every man who receives the Father's grace through the Son Jesus, Father and Son come and make their home within.[10]

God's absolute act of selfless love is not a New Testament tack on. The Lamb was slain before the foundation of the world.[11] In God's heart this was a done deal before you and I were thought of. Think of it, the glory of God was made flesh, crucified, and raised up again, all so you and I can live His intention. Jesus gave up His own glory to pay the sacrifice for man's sin of unbelief and living "my" way.[12]

Raised in a Christian home, I grew up with the teaching that I needed my sins forgiven in order to go to heaven, and I had to be sanctified so I would do all the right things. Although it probably was not proclaimed in these exact words, my interpretation was that all anger would be gone, I'd love everybody, all my problems would be solved, and, if I did the right things, God would be pleased. I'd have the desires of my heart, and many people would come to Jesus! I, too, like the Israelites, wanted Jesus. I wanted Jesus plus my own way, Jesus plus the blessings of a good marriage, perfect kids, successful ministry, and beautiful home. The list was endless. I, like them, wanted a God who would perform for me and fulfill my wants. Unless Jesus is my only center and source, nothing is truly glorious, only a delusion of my own making. "For we have made falsehood our refuge and we have concealed ourselves with deception" (Isaiah 28:15b NASB).

When Jesus became enough for me in 1999, He forgave the past and filled me with the ultimate gift of grace, the fullness of His Holy Spirit. He is presently filling me with the holiness of God and pouring into me the selfless agape love of Calvary. This is His glory!

Jesus said it is expedient that He return to His Father so He can send the Holy Spirit who will allow us to share in His glory! Incredible! Impossible? No! This is why Jesus came! Yes, Jesus is enough to forgive past sin, enough to cleanse the heart of sin, enough to be the power to turn from sin, but the ultimate purpose of His coming was to impart to man His same Glory—the fullness of all that He Is—Holy Love!

For years I desired to know Him, but I never realized that to know Him is to have His glory. I strived out of my flesh to be what only Jesus is, then I'd put the tag on the work giving Him the glory. God receives glory only when I allow His glory to be the center and the source from which the motivation and word is given. To truly know Him as husband knows his wife, two becoming one flesh, is when I choose to allow the Holy Spirit to permeate my own spirit with all of His fullness that we might be truly one.

"I have given them the glory you gave me, so they may be one as we are one. I am in them and you are in me. May they experience such perfect unity that the world will know that you sent me and that you love them as much as you love me" (John 17:22-23).

Oh, how I praise Father, Son, and Holy Spirit for His persistent, jealous love that allowed my life to come crumbling down so I could finally be aware something was missing. Not a thing, a One! I lived Christianity as a newly conceived baby but had never realized God didn't intend for me just to be born of His glory but to remain in His glory so I might live His glory to a lost world.

This has been a difficult year full of disappointments, delays, dreadful news, and very little evidence of the answers to prayer offered so faithfully for years. Amazingly, the glory of the Lord has never been more real even though there is little feeling of success, very few miracles on the horizon, and not much fruit seen from the sowing of His Word. Do you realize that the God of

Glory is not based on feelings, man's logic, or His miraculous deeds? God's Glory isn't about tangible or temporal blessings. Allow me to remind you, the blessings are the overflow of His glory. God's glory gives me His mind, the mind of Christ,[13] to make decisions that are for the sake of another's spiritual wellbeing rather than looking out for myself. When I draw near to Him, I receive His all-sufficient supply of the riches of His glory. I need not look to another person, buy, eat, or act from impulse or form addictions to temporarily make me feel better. Jesus is enough!

His Holy Spirit brings to you all of who He is with all of the heavenly riches out of His Glory. "For God wanted them to know that the riches and glory of Christ are for you Gentiles, too. And this is the secret: Christ lives in you. This gives you assurance of sharing His glory" (Colossians 1:27). His Spirit is the promise we can share in His glory. Everything else He provides are red roses out of the overflow of Who He is—absolutely enough!

Most of us come to Him hoping He came to give us back Paradise. He did not. He came to give us the presence of the One whom we lack so that you and I might live His Glory! The question is, "Is Jesus enough for you?"

For you died to this life, and your real life is hidden with Christ in God. And when Christ, who is your life, is revealed to the whole world, you will share in all his glory (Colossians 3:3-4).

Chapter 4

I Beheld His Glory

Tricia Maxey

LORD, *we show our trust in you by obeying your laws; our heart's desire is to glorify your name (Isaiah 26:8).*

The first Come to the Fire conference had come and gone before I heard of it, but when I saw the pictures and heard the reports, I made a mental note to attend the next one. So in 2007, a friend and I made our way to the second Come to the Fire.

I entered the door, and instantly the theme of the year came alive to me—"Behold His Glory!" I was welcomed by beautiful, worshipful piano music that immediately brought my heart to praise. The moment I heard the music, I said to my friend, "I would know that piano playing anywhere! That is Carol Ketchum!" Sure enough, there was Carol playing the prelude music. Carol had been my pastor's wife several years before, but I was unaware that she was on the Come to the Fire council.

That night, she gave her testimony. The following afternoon at the beginning of the healing service, each attendee was given a tiny gift box containing a piece of paper on which we were to write a prayer request. Then we were to remove a small layer of cotton; under it was another piece of paper with a Scripture that had been prayed over for us. We were to remove it and place the prayer request in the bottom of the box symbolic of releasing that need totally into God's care! When I pulled out my Scripture, I couldn't believe my eyes; it was Isaiah 41:10, the very verse Carol shared in her testimony the evening before. After the service Carol was waving to me to come see her verse. She exclaimed, "Look! Look at my Scripture verse in my box!" It was, of course, Isaiah 41:10. I said, "Well, look at mine!" We hugged, laughed, did a little happy dance, and cried a few tears! Oh, our amazing God loves to lavish us with surprising gifts!

When we opened our boxes, I looked over at my friend Martha, and she had tears in her eyes. She and her husband had sold his business and moved to a farm to raise a special breed of cattle. Things had gone great for a while, but the past two years the land had experienced drought. The streams were drying up, and it looked as though the cattle were going to have to be sold at great loss. When she pulled out her verse, it read 2 Kings 3:16-17: "This is what the LORD says, I will fill this valley with pools of water....You will see neither wind nor rain, yet this valley will be filled with water, and you, your cattle, and your other animals will drink" (II Kings 3:16-17 NIV). Through tears she said, "I have to call Larry."

As we left the conference, I could not begin to fathom what God had in store for me throughout the next eight years because of CTTF connections and interactions.

I immediately began to see God work like never before in my life. I didn't want to miss any of what He had for me and made plans to return to CTTF in 2008.

Although I was looking forward to it, the year had dealt some blows in my life, and heaviness accompanied me. Some doubts had moved in; circumstances were not better, but worse; and so my attitude was not the best, to say the least. You could say my attitude had become, "Okay, Lord, I am here. I came. Move me if you can!" Certainly I am not proud of this now!

I did enjoy the services and the music, but, honestly, I can't say I was feeling a real part of the conference at that point; however, Friday afternoon things changed drastically. As we entered the service, we were given a Sharpie and a small stone. At the end of the service, the speaker, Rondy Smith, explained that God has given us each a name, and He calls us by name; He loves us; He knows all about us!

Suddenly, I was in full sarcasm. "Oh yeah," I said, "You know my name; how hard is that? Patricia?" Oh, but then Rondy asked us to spread out across the sanctuary to get alone and pray, asking God to tell us His name for us. Still in a slightly sarcastic mode, but agreeing within me to try this, I moved to a spot alone. I began to tell the Lord how disappointing my year had been. I was in a full-fledged pity party when suddenly I realized that large sanctuary was hushed, pin drop silent! It got my attention! I said, "Okay, Lord, if you have a name for me, what is it?" And I waited.

I don't know how long the silence lasted, but I do know that the first thing I heard several minutes later from the far right side was "Glory! Glory to God!" Then from the center I heard joyful laughter!

I saw a woman dance down the aisle before the Lord! I heard sobbing from my left! Joyful sounds replaced the silence! Then I thought I heard a whisper! I kept listening and said, "Lord, was that You? Were you giving me my name?"

I listened again, and God spoke to my spirit! "Years ago, I gave you four words: Encouragement, Caring, Compassion, and Hope. I told you to wait, and in My time I would explain them. Later I called you to a ministry of divine appointments, using encouragement, caring, compassion, and hope. You followed my leading until you allowed a human being's words to cause you to take your eyes and ears off Me. This gave the evil one a foothold of discouragement, and you dropped that ministry. I didn't remove it from you nor change My mind. You walked away. There is still so much more I have for you to do in My kingdom work, but you have to put your eyes back on Me and tune your ears to hear My voice."

By now, I was weeping, listening intently, and asked Him again, "What is my name, Lord?"

I heard clearly, "Your name is Divinely Appointed." I wept! Then I picked up my Sharpie and stone and wrote on it my God-given name. I made a new commitment to follow Him wherever He would lead and meet His divine appointments whenever, wherever, and however He planned them for me! I vowed to walk through the doors He opened! God made me a promise that day, and I decided to trust Him completely! That year, at Come to the Fire, I had experienced once again the truth of the theme "Discover Your Promise."

I have continued to attend every Come to the Fire since, and each year the theme has come alive for me. God has spoken to me in specific ways and deepened My walk with Him while expanding the ministry He has ordained.

My new life theme song is the title song written for the 2014 Come to the Fire CD:

I will worship at the front lines, bringing light to the darkness,
Declaring who You are; Your power is my confidence.
I will worship at the front lines, singing praise through the long night,
Trusting in the Truth, knowing this is not my fight!
I will worship, I will worship at the front lines.[1]

Now, may the God of peace make you holy in every way, and may your whole spirit and soul and body be kept blameless until our Lord Jesus Christ comes again. God will make this happen, for He who calls you is faithful (I Thessalonians 5:23-24).

Fireflies

CTTF Attendees

Firefly Leader

I attended the first Come to the Fire alone; however, in 2007, I brought a group of ladies from my church, my two daughters, and my sister from another state. Friday night in our hotel, we shared with one another what God had revealed to us at CTTF. On the way home Saturday afternoon, my pastor husband called to ask about my reflections on the conference, and before our conversation ended, he invited our ladies and me to give testimonies in the worship service the next morning. My ladies were full of joy and already prepared from our sharing time Friday night. At the close of the Sunday morning CTTF presentation, it was obvious the men were hungry for the Fire to be outpoured on them as well. Someone in our group soon gave us the name Fireflies which we joyfully claimed.

As a result of Come to the Fire, I was able to start a Lydia Prayer Group with business women in my community. This group had started as a book study on leadership; however, after attending CTTF, I began to sense that God wanted this diverse group of ladies to do more than study leadership. I began to pray for God to open their hearts and give them a hunger for Him. Within two months, one of the ladies asked if I would lead in prayer and perhaps we could begin to pray at each meeting! Thus, our Lydia Prayer Group began with a bank president, Chamber of Commerce president, director of an outreach program for at risk children, store owner, educator, and a fundraiser for non-profit companies. We meet in the back room of a store in the shopping center in our community. Our prayer goal is to pray for our leaders, educators, and churches, and for God's glory to be evident in the businesses in our town. We have seen miracles in our community and in our personal lives. We often praise God for the privilege of interceding for our town.

Light Reflector

When my pastor's wife returned from the first Come to the Fire Conference, I wanted what she had and could hardly wait to go myself. After I attended, I invited my daughter to go with me the next year. She responded eagerly because she said, "My mother came home from Come to the Fire changed. It changed my dad; it changed me; it changed our entire family," and it is true!

Light Receiver

I have to admit I was skeptical at first about attending Come to the Fire. I wasn't interested in another women's conference with a parade of speakers meant to entertain, taking the listener through emotional highs and lows without much substance in between. That's not at all what I found at this conference; it was all about Jesus! I'm so thankful for my experiences at each Come to the Fire

Conference. I'm glad I listened to the prompting of the Holy Spirit! Oh, what I would have missed out on if I had hesitated!

Light Penetrated

My first CTTF was overwhelmingly refreshing. I was running at a survival pace and was reading and praying but not reaching a fulfilling moment. Upon arriving at CTTF, I had the opportunity to spend one-on-one time with God. My desire and life structure changed. Little did I know that after my first CTTF I would be walking through the valley of death with preparations for a liver transplant. I believe my experience at CTTF prepared me and helped me become strong enough in my relationship with God to endure, knowing He was by my side.

Light Blazing

God changed my life dramatically. God became so real and close to me.

Part III

Discover Your Promise

By Aletha Hinthorn

...you will receive the gift of the Holy Spirit. The promise is for you and your children and for all who are far off... (Acts 2:38-39 NIV).

His purposes for having a holy people go far beyond our own joy and satisfaction. He declared that the cleansing of His people would be so that "the nations will know that I am the LORD, declares the Sovereign LORD, when I show myself holy through you before their eyes" (Ezekiel 36:23 NIV). Amazingly, God intends to show His holiness to others through us!

"The Lord will establish you as his holy people, as he promised you on oath, if you keep the commands of the LORD your God and walk in obedience to him. Then all the peoples on earth will see that you are called by the name of the LORD" (Deuteronomy 28:9 NIV).

Chapter 5

Mind Changing Discoveries

Ani Simmons[1]

Do not conform any longer to the pattern of this world, but be transformed by the renewing of your mind. Then you will be able to test and approve what God's will is—his good, pleasing, and perfect will (Romans 12:2).

I came to my first Come to the Fire conference in 2007 while I was in the midst of a traumatic school year. My mother had attended the first conference in 2006 and came home determined to take others with her the next year. I am glad that included me. We were scurrying into the session late on Friday morning when I heard my name called from the platform. Patsy Lewis was saying, "If Ani and Monda Simmons and Rhonda McGinnis are in the audience, will you please come to the platform?" She wanted to interview us spontaneously about our Lydia Prayer groups.

My mom had challenged the ladies of our church to become part of the Lydia Prayer movement, and we had more than fifty ladies involved in various Lydia groups around the Dallas area praying for God's Spirit to be poured out in our families, churches, city, and the world. Several met in homes; one was formed in a prison; another group of young mothers met at a Sonic Drive-in and prayed in the car as they sipped cherry limeades. My sister was leading a teen Lydia Prayer group in the Atlanta area, and I had my teacher group. We each shared a piece of our story as Patsy interviewed us; then she called the assembly to pray with partners as we formed a huge Lydia Prayer group right there at the conference. At my first Come to the Fire experience, I was challenged to forgive and live life with Jesus alone and no plusses—not Jesus plus control, plus my way, plus anything. Jesus is enough!

At the 2008 conference, we were given instructions to ask God what our new name was to be. I went to be by myself in the prayer room, which was strangely deserted. As I sat there, instrumental worship music was playing softly, and I started thinking of lots of names. My problem was that I was thinking of the names that I'd given myself, the world had given me, and that the enemy had made me think were the only names I deserved: Controlling, Alone, Unloved, Unwanted, Inadequate, Mine, Afraid, Depressed, Bitter, No, Can't, Ugly, Weak, Held, Prisoner, Self-Centered, and Lost. I quit writing down the negative names because I was so sad and defeated thinking I would never have even one new name.

I cried out to the Lord, "Help me!" Just at that moment I heard the song "I Surrender All" playing in the background, and I looked at the first name on my list, Controlling, and I wanted so much not to be that anymore.

"Lord, is this my new name?" I prayed as I wrote next to Controlling my new name, Surrendered. My pencil continued to write new names as I wept: Surrounded, Loved, Wanted, Enough, His, Bold, Joyful, Sweet, Yes, Will, Beautiful, Powerful, Released, Free, Self-less, and Found. The Lord had not given me just one new name; He had helped me see myself as He sees me: Beautiful.

When I told my sister about this, I understood and felt fully, for the very first time in my life, that God, the Creator of the Universe, loved me! I wept tears of joy for what that knowledge meant for my future and mourning for the years of love the enemy had helped me steal from myself. In the communion service the next day, I was overcome with His love for me as I partook of the elements representing how much He has always loved me; no communion has ever been so precious.

I surrendered my life at the altar with my mother helping me to finally realize that no amount of knowledge I could gain would help me figure anything out for myself, like how to purify my heart, soul, and mind. In Joy Griffin's testimony, someone told her she "had gotten just enough Jesus to make her miserable." That's how I felt all the time: miserable. I realized I'm not smart enough to ever figure out how to be enough, do enough, or love enough to be worthy of God's love. He just loves us and purifies us; we can't do that for ourselves, no matter how smart we are.

I left that conference as Surrendered and Beautiful, my new names, and went home determined to remain surrendered. However, I was in the midst of finishing my Master's degree and changing careers at age thirty-seven. My life was a minefield of reasons to try to take control back. I began shutting myself off from everyone and everything; then I wouldn't be tempted to take control—so I thought. I gave up my name Beautiful and became Ugly again. I hated it; I was miserable.

By shutting myself off from the temptation to take control, I had done that very thing. As a visual learner, I realized I needed to somehow visually give my mind to Christ so he could give me his when I was ready for it.

I saw a commercial for a toothbrush that is effective for those who don't have a flip-top head, as none of us do! I thought, "That's what I need: a flip-top skull so I can just reach in and take out my mind to give it to Christ." I pictured myself doing just that! As gruesome as it sounds, it's the only way I could begin to truly surrender. I then realized that I needed to surrender every part of myself: my hands, my feet, my mouth, my eyes, my ears, my stomach, my heart, my stomach—again! (That one is a work in progress!)

I have taken the old hymns "Be Thou My Vision" and "Take My Life" as my mantras when I feel out of control and want to take my mind back from Christ. Why would I want to give up the chance to have the mind of Christ?[2] I choose to surrender to Him daily!

...no one can know God's thoughts except God's own Spirit. And we have received God's Spirit (not the world's spirit), so we can know the wonderful things God has freely given us....Those who are spiritual can evaluate all things, but they themselves cannot be evaluated by others. For, "Who can know the LORD's thoughts? Who knows enough to teach him?" But we understand these things, for we have the mind of Christ (I Corinthians 2:11, 15-16).

Chapter 6

Promises Discovered–Fear Released

Cheryl Roland[1]

I am leaving you with a gift—peace of mind and heart, and the peace I give is a gift the world cannot give. So don't be troubled or afraid (John 4:27).

What could be more thrilling? Generous friends trusted us with their shiny, late model motor home, complete with microwave, clean beds and a shower. The girls, now ages eight and five, were beyond ecstatic as they proudly announced to curious neighbors eyeing the RV that we were going on vacation.

With bags packed, favorite foods purchased, and special activities all mapped out, each of us toured the RV, anticipating an early morning departure. David, Kari, and Cassie all agreed it was the best, most perfect plan imaginable. However, when I stepped into the camper, my airways constricted. My skin crawled as my pounding heart regretfully expressed doubts that this vacation would be any different than the rest. Once again my irrational germ phobias and unfounded fears created complications.

David made several attempts to pacify me by wiping down every surface with bleach water. Finally, in kindness, but with a firm voice, he declared the camper "clean enough," and we all headed out the next morning. Excitement was an understatement as the girls each claimed their space and made themselves right at home, but the family seemed oblivious to my lack of joy—or were they just used to it? To be honest, I was at my wit's end. How could they be so careless, so comfortable?

Unlike having a quick wit, which linguists say is the ability to find a creative solution to a problem, my "wit quit" as worry consumed all sense of humor and anticipation of family fun. According to pastor and author David Wilkerson, "Wit's end, simply means, having lost or exhausted any possibility of perceiving or thinking of a way out...."[2]

The Psalmist describes sailors at their wit's end when a storm threatened their lives (Psalm 107:27). The Douay-Rheims Bible says, "All their wisdom was swallowed up in fear." But, the passage continues, "Then they cried out to the Lord in their trouble, and He brought them out of their distress" (Psalm 107:28 NIV).

The storms of anger, fear, and frustration were threatening my sanity and our family health. Why didn't God hear my cry? For nearly nineteen years I suffered from mild to severe anxiety attacks. The fear of danger, germs, dirt, and disaster robbed my joy and sometimes immobilized me. Healthy fear is necessary for self-preservation, but I suffered from exaggerated distress and unfounded panic that eroded my confidence and stifled my ability to laugh and love.

I'm not sure why or how it all began, but obsessive fear became more obvious when, after years of infertility, we were blessed with a precious baby girl. Kari totally and completely captured my devotion, and all of my energies were spent protecting her and meeting her needs. Three years later, another sweet, pink bundle of blessings arrived. Cassie was premature, requiring extra attention, but perfect in every way. Now with two little ones, it became nearly impossible to maintain the extensive regimen of protective care I thought necessary.

As the girls grew, I treasured their innocence and celebrated their every accomplishment but continued to carefully monitor their safety. What if they were abducted or became gravely ill because I failed to protect them? There was also a chance they could embarrass me by behaving poorly or disregarding my standards of cleanliness. Sometimes the girls were courageous enough to say with a smile, "God made dirt. Dirt won't hurt!" Sadly, anger was my automatic response when they failed to comply. David, a wise, godly husband and father, never ceased to support me but gently softened negative responses with grace.

David was the pastor of a thriving church. Somehow I met the demands of ministry without revealing my limits. Keeping up appearances seemed to be the safest approach. One moment I made decisions based on sound reason, and the next moment fear ruled. An honest admission would have pierced my fortress resulting in embarrassment, wounded pride, and a damaged reputation. So, the magnitude of my fears was reserved for our immediate family, and even then, I often suffered silently because I didn't want to appear weak or out of control. David recognized the potential that fear was stifling and always reinforced every hint of personal growth.

I grieve over the lost opportunities as perfectionism and unrealistic expectations dampened the most precious years of our lives. I grieve over my lack of confidence and jealousy of other women that prevented me from totally embracing friendships.

I knew my actions and reactions were displeasing to God and often felt I had grieved the Holy Spirit. Could Jesus heal my hollow heart? Theologian J.H. Jowett suggests Christians should bear "the marks of heavenly love and grace."[3] Or do we instead bear the marks of "dingy things, stingy things, ungracious things, things gathered from the streets of ingratitude and the haunts of discontent?"[4]

Fear was competing with faith. More often than not, I was ungrateful and discontented. My heart was divided as "self" competed for the throne that was intended for Jesus Christ alone. Oswald Chambers asks, "What kind of mean little imps have been looking in *on you*, (italics mine) and saying, 'now what are you going to do...?'"[5]

Fear threatens love, joy, peace and patience. Fear robs us of kindness, goodness, faithfulness, gentleness and self-control.[6] When my "self" was in control, those dingy things, stingy things, ungracious things took precedence over a happy heart that freely expressed love for God and others. From my "mouth came blessing and cursing."[7] My heart was divided, and my loyalties to Jesus Christ were compromised because of unhealthy fear.

Fear comes in many forms. Situation fears deal with circumstances such as anger, germs, illness, rodents, financial loss, heights, and small spaces, etc. Another category of fear involves the ego; this would include the fear of failure, embarrassment, rejection, and vulnerability. Recently, I learned of an acrostic for ego: Edging God Out! I was living proof that if left unchecked, both situation and ego fears multiply in silence until there is no room for God. I was at my wit's end.

Oswald Chambers expressed remorse, "Lord, I have had misgivings about Thee. I have not believed in Thy wits apart from my own. I have not believed in Thine almighty power apart from my finite understanding of it."[8] Carefully read his prayer again. Can you relate? Fear mounts, and waves of worry threaten to destroy us when we lean on our own understanding and respond to difficulties in life thinking we know better than Almighty God.

Finally, the end of my wits was a glorious beginning as I turned to "the God of all flesh" who asks, "Is anything too hard for Me?" (Jeremiah 32:27 KJV). Our great Counselor, Comforter, and Friend extended an irresistible invitation to me, "Come now, and let us reason together. Though your sins are like scarlet, they shall be as white as snow. Though they are red like crimson, they shall be as wool" (Isaiah 1:18 NKJV).

Oh, the love of Jesus! He wooed me into His presence and revealed that my fear was rooted in pride! I was self-absorbed, self-seeking, self-sufficient, self-destructive, and filled with self-pity. I fell before the Father, and the Lord Jesus Christ, merciful Savior, cleansed me of sin and self! When I surrendered, the precious Holy Spirit blessed me with "power, love and a sound mind!" (II Timothy 1:7 NKJV)

Immediately I felt alive! The world seemed transformed into brilliant colors, and all heaven rejoiced in my celebrated surrender. Our family began to notice the joyful difference as I more readily declared my love for God, love for them, and burden for others who were living in fear and doubt. Through the power and profound grace of God's precious Holy Spirit, I began to reflect the mind of Christ, the mouth of Christ, and the mood of Christ!

His Word became my flesh, as every passage took on new meaning and fresh application. In obedience to the Lord, I searched the Scriptures for passages that dealt with fear. I recorded His promises and claimed them as my own. This is my prayer and praise, "Teach me your way, LORD, that I may rely on your faithfulness; give me an undivided heart, that I may fear your name. I will praise you, Lord my God, with all my heart; I will glorify your name forever. For great is your love toward me; you have delivered me from the depths." (Psalm 86:11-13 NIV).

Since that day of absolute surrender to the cleansing power of God's Holy Spirit, I have experienced indescribable joy and peace! When the enemy challenges my faith, and fear rears its ugly head, Jesus is my strength and song! Elmer Towns describes it well: "When your desperation for God exceeds your fear, then nothing in life can scare you."9

Remember, "The name of the Lord is a strong tower; the (consistently) righteous man (upright and in right standing with God) runs into it and is safe, high (above evil) and strong!" (Proverbs 18:10 AMP).

What does it take to stay consistently righteous, upright, and in right standing with God?

• Prayer and Praise: I learned that self-effort always ends in fear and failure. It is "the very God of peace who sanctifies us through and through" (I Thessalonians 5:23 NIV). When we acknowledge God's greatness and surrender to His Holy Spirit, we receive joy in His presence, power over sin, and love enough to intercede for others. Prayer is simply acknowledging our own limitations and God's boundless, inexhaustible power. Praise Him!

• Fasting: Almighty God threw open the windows of heaven and poured out a blessing so great I could not contain it.[10] Fasting food was one way I could express my gratitude for His healing touch. Through regular fasting and prayer, we can experience deeper fellowship with Jesus who keeps His promises. "Blessed are those who hunger and thirst for righteousness, for they will be filled" (Matthew 5:6 NIV).

• Worship God corporately and privately: Seek the support of other Christians through regular church attendance, the fellowship of believers, and small group accountability. "As iron sharpens iron, so one friend sharpens another" (Proverbs 27:17 NIV). In private worship I have found that journaling, reading Scriptures out loud, and incorporating music have blessed and strengthened my walk with the Spirit.

• Study God's Word: I have discovered undeniable strength through the fervent study of the Scriptures. Richard Foster in his excellent book *Celebration of Discipline* explains it well.

"Many Christians remain in bondage to fears and anxieties simply because they do not avail themselves to the Discipline of study. They may be faithful in church attendance and earnest in fulfilling their religious duties, and still they are not changed. I am not here speaking only of those who are going through mere religious forms, but of those who are genuinely seeking to worship and obey Jesus Christ as Lord and Master. They may sing with gusto, pray in the Spirit, live as obediently as they know, even receive divine visions and revelations, and yet the terror of their lives remains unchanged. Why? Because they have never taken up one of the central ways God uses to change us: study. Jesus made it unmistakably clear that the knowledge of the truth will set us free. 'You will know the truth, and the truth will make you free'" (John 8:32).[11]

Hallelujah! I'm so glad Jesus set me free and continues to fill my journey with love, joy, and peace as I stand on the promises that I have discovered in His Word!

So we can say with confidence, The LORD is my helper, so I will have no fear (Hebrews 13:6a).

Broken and Poured Out

CTTF Attendees

I was sorely in need of time away to refresh and hear from God. I heard a women's event advertised on the radio here in Kansas City, but it was expensive, and we were selling personal possessions to pay medical bills. I just couldn't ask my husband to take on one more expense. Then my friend emailed me about Come to the Fire. She said it was free, and the subject was the Holy Spirit. I had been crying out for help to experience God's power in my life and ministry, so I immediately registered.

I went to the conference feeling weary, battered and unworthy to serve. I left broken and poured out, an offering to God. My heart is "squeaky clean." I understand the concept of sin for the first time. I am filled with the Holy Spirit; my marriage is healed; and I am hungry to learn how to intercede in prayer.

I am bolder in my daily life. Recently we held a prayer meeting at my office with our office manager's permission, and I'm thinking of ways to connect my extended family in prayer through the Internet.

My friend who sent me the information about CTTF and I are determined to bring the fire home to our church. Our pastor approved the purchase of the DVDs so we are planning a Come to the Fire conference for the ladies here.

One last thing, it grieved me not to have more money to put in the offering plate, so I prayed about it. God showed me that I could ask friends and family to donate to CTTF as a gift to me for my birthday, Christmas and Mother's Day. I can't think of anything I would like more! Come to the Fire Ministries will be in my prayers regularly.

Part IV

Receive Your Inheritance

Aletha Hinthorn

...receive forgiveness of sins and an inheritance among those who are sanctified through faith (Acts 26:18 NKJV).

God promised the Israelites that their inheritance would be the land of Canaan—a land of rest. In Canaan they would have rest because God would give them victory over all their enemies. But God had something greater in mind than a physical place of rest in Canaan. He was picturing for us the spiritual rest and the victorious life we have when we live in Christ. Jesus invites us to receive our inheritance: "God's promise of entering His rest still stands" (Hebrews 4:1).

"Furthermore, because we are united with Christ, we have received an inheritance from God, for he chose us in advance, and he makes everything work out according to his plan. The Spirit is God's guarantee that he will give us the inheritance he promised and that he has purchased us

to be his own people. He did this so we would praise and glorify him" (Ephesians 1:11, 14).

Chapter 7

I Received My True Inheritance

Jan Wilson[1]

The LORD is close to the brokenhearted; he rescues those whose spirits are crushed. But the LORD will redeem those who serve him. No one who takes refuge in him will be condemned (Psalm 34:18, 22).

I volunteered to work at the book tables at the first Come to the Fire conference as a favor to a new friend, having no clue what I was getting myself into. I was shy and fearful and didn't know anyone; I couldn't believe I had actually volunteered to be there. I almost didn't stay, but I am thankful I did because God had a plan to heal my heart of the pain and shame that I had been carrying as long as I could remember. It was easy to believe in God's love and forgiveness for other people. But I feared I had run too far from Him to receive His compassion for myself. I lived in fear of getting close to people. My internal mantra was, "If people only knew the real me..."

The "real me" began in a small town in the Midwest, born to a single mother with six children by four different fathers. Before I was a year old, my mother abandoned me to an elderly woman named Annie who had been babysitting my siblings and me. Annie was my world, the only mother I knew. I lived in a small house with Annie and her sick husband, and we called her Grandma.

Annie was extremely poor by the world's standards but poured all of her love into me. She taught me, by example, kindness and compassion, frequently read the Bible to me at night, and prayed with me before I went to bed. She taught me "Jesus Loves Me" and "Everyday with Jesus Is Sweeter Than the Day Before;" however, we didn't go to church except for Easter. Annie made every day an adventure, and I loved her fiercely. She didn't spoil me but took care of my basic needs, loved me unconditionally, and always cried when she had to discipline me. Annie had one great fear in her life—that someday my mother would suddenly show up and try to take me away from her.

When I was seven, I came home from school one day to learn that Annie was very ill. Three days later, she died from a heart aneurysm. It rocked my world. I felt so terrified and abandoned. The only constant in my life was gone. Who would take care of me? I was taken to her son's house where a lot of relatives were gathered to discuss what to do with me. Nobody wanted to take me in, but it was finally decided that I would go live with Annie's oldest son and wife who lived close by.

For the next two years, I felt like an unwanted guest in their home. They had a sixteen-year-old son with Down's syndrome, and I was an additional burden. I had nice clothes and my own room in a comfortable house in the suburbs, but I never felt as if I were wanted or loved. The husband slept days and worked nights. The wife was a very angry person. If I got something out of the fridge without asking or made a mess in the house, she would chase me to the living room and beat me with a belt and her fists while yelling at me. I remember always being terrified of doing something to incur her wrath.

The summer I was nine, I was playing alone outside when a car drove up and parked across the street from our house. I never remember having seen my mother, but as the driver got out of the car and started up the driveway, I ran into the house screaming and crying that my mother was outside to take me away. I hid behind the couch, and my caretaker went to see who was ringing the doorbell. I was right. It was my mother, and she wanted to visit with me. She had come looking for me and discovered from neighbors that Annie had died. After I was assured no one was taking me anywhere, I calmed down and went downstairs to talk with her. At the end of that summer, my mother asked me to come live with her and my siblings. I didn't feel loved where I was living, so I thought it would be better to go live with my mother. Surely she would love me. She was, after all, my mother.

I got to my mother's house to find that there were seven people and an ever changing assortment of cats and dogs all living in a small, two bedroom house with no working bathroom. I slept on a baby mattress on the living room floor. The chaos and filth were overwhelming.

We regularly attended a small church on Sunday mornings, and at the age of nine, I asked Jesus into my heart.

I was in the fourth grade when I went to live with my real family, and my mother managed to keep us in Christian schools around the city, moving on to the next school when it was discovered that we couldn't pay the tuition. She worked very hard at keeping up an outward appearance that we were a "normal" family. Behind closed doors, however, my mother was an angry, unhappy woman, and for reasons still unknown to me, she focused her rage on my next older sister and me in the forms of physical and verbal abuse. We never knew what would trigger her anger and lived on edge waiting for the next time she would throw one of us against a wall and beat us with whatever was close at hand.

My mother lost her job when I was twelve and became even angrier with life. She spiraled into a deep depression and never got another job. Food was often non-existent, and had it not been for the free lunch program at school, some days we wouldn't have eaten at all. We had no running water, no plumbing, and no heat because there was no money for such things.

When I was thirteen, God sent a bus ministry worker from a large church to our door, and I started attending this church by myself. Church life became my sanctuary away from the craziness of my home life. I poured myself into church work. You name it, I volunteered. My church family knew nothing of my family life; I was too ashamed to tell anyone. During this time, I started working nights and weekends at the age of fifteen to help put food on the table. I never saw the paychecks as my mother would intercept them in the mail.

When I turned seventeen, I finally decided to tell our youth pastor the truth about my life because I badly needed help. I told him everything, even about the physical abuse and sexual molestation that had been happening. He didn't believe me. He thought I was exaggerating. He had met my mother, and she seemed like a loving mother to him. I was stunned. I had attended that youth department for four years, was heavily involved in various ministries, loved God, attended their Christian school, and worked to pay for school by cleaning the church when I wasn't working my real job. I made straight A's and was one of the leaders in the teen department. I didn't even hold hands with my church boyfriend! And yet, the pastor didn't believe me! Hope died in me that day. As soon as I graduated from high school that year, I ran away from home and from God.

I married a man I did not love, became pregnant on my honeymoon, and gave birth to a beautiful daughter. She was amazing—finally someone I could love who loved me in return. She was the one joy in my life. My husband was not good at providing for even our most basic needs, so when my daughter was two years old, I went to work to support the family. Work was hard to come by in this small town, and when I did get a job, I "fell in love" with a co-worker, left my husband and daughter, and ran off with this man to another state. The only way I felt I could punish myself for the sin of leaving my husband was to leave my daughter also. Far above anything that was ever done to me, leaving my child would prove to be the deepest wound in my soul.

As you can probably guess, my life didn't work out like a fairy tale with this man either. My mother died when I was thirty. My second marriage ended within a year after that. I occasionally had contact with my daughter but didn't see her much more than one week each year because of the distance and because I felt like I had already damaged enough of her life.

Throughout the years that I was running from God, He continued placing people and situations in my life to remind me that He was still there. My younger brother and his wife, who lived their Christianity, never gave up on me.

During the four years I lived alone after my second divorce, I managed to go back to college and get a degree. Once I graduated, I had a sudden, urgent desire to go back to the town where I had grown up. I believe God placed that desire within me. So I quit my job, left my friends, and moved back to my hometown.

Within three days of arriving, I landed a great job as a paralegal. The first person I met there was a Christian, a pastor's wife. God isn't always subtle; I so love His sense of humor. It took time, but my heart began to turn toward the things of God again.

God began restoring the lean years. I developed an amazing relationship with my daughter. She is now married and has two beautiful children, and, wonder of wonders, she trusts me with her children. God led me to an amazing man that loves and serves Him, and we have now been married for fourteen years. My husband and I attend a large, local church. In the last four years, through church and Come to the Fire, God has placed some amazing, godly women in my life that have been Jesus to me; however, I was still carrying the secret shame of my past like a dead weight. Only a few people knew the truth about my former life, and I certainly had been careful not to share my story with anyone from my new life.

Each year as I served at Come to the Fire, I was careful not to attend too many of the conference sessions. I realize now it was because I knew God wanted to work in my heart and life, but I held on to the bondage of my past; and although I hated it, I didn't dare let myself believe that I could live any other way.

By the time I got to the conference in Nashville, I had managed to avoid most of the sessions by being too busy at the book tables. Finally, on Saturday morning, one of my co-volunteers literally made me go into the session. Just before communion, we were standing and singing. I can't even remember the song, but suddenly I knew I couldn't go on another minute the way I had been living. I cried out to God and told Him I was tired, exhausted from the weight of the pain and shame I had accumulated and carried on my back since childhood. I didn't want to live like this any longer. God heard my cry.

I didn't tell anyone what had happened. We finished the conference, packed up the tables, and went to dinner with plans to drive home the following morning. I awoke at 5:00 a.m. and realized I had been crying in my sleep. I heard a chorus of a song we had sung at the conference the day before ringing loudly in my head: "My chains are gone; I've been set free." I couldn't stop sobbing from sheer relief and joy. I felt as though the weight of the world had been lifted from my body and soul. I joyfully began telling people; I started with my dear husband and moved on to Aletha Hinthorn and the other people who had been waiting for us downstairs in the hotel.

God is continuing to heal my heart, and I have a renewed sense of His love and plans for my life. God has forgiven me, and I am learning to forgive myself. I share these deeply personal things so people will know there is nothing that can separate us from the love of Christ. He is always there, continually wooing us to Himself. I still cry a lot, but they are tears of gratitude that God doesn't leave us where we are.

Four years have passed since I shared my testimony at CTTF in Grove City in 2011. I am happy to tell you of my continuing story, as doing so is to tell of His goodness and grace.

Over these past few years, God has continued to bless me with healing in my mind and spirit and has taught me several "heart truths." To me, a heart truth is something that you know in your head and believe to be true, but when you understand it with your heart, it becomes a living reality in your daily life in everything you do.

Life has not been without its challenges. Last year, my best friend and husband, Carl, had quadruple bypass surgery in July, followed by months of complications, and then another ten-day hospital stay over Thanksgiving.

During that time, I learned, and came to believe with my whole heart, that I could rely on God for everything. He became my strength, my comforter, my provision, my peace. I received a confidence from God that He would provide anything and everything that we needed, even before we knew what that would be. No matter what happened, I simply had to rest in Him. If you knew me at all, you would know that rest has never been in my vocabulary, so it was such a relief when I came to the end of my strength and resources and fully understood that God had, and continues to have, every detail under control.

Looking back, there were many miracles during that time, including selling our house five times in nine months! That might sound crazy, but we had been in the process of selling our home when Carl became ill, and four of the five buyers gave us substantial deposits at the time of contract. Then each of them walked away at various stages of the process for different reasons and insisted we keep their deposit money! We even gained friends on two of those deals, and one couple brought food to us when Carl came home from the hospital! We could not have planned that ourselves; only the great God of the universe could have made that happen! As I write this a full year later, I am thankful to be able to report that by God's grace, Carl is doing well today.

I have also come to fully know that God is my biggest champion. A few days ago, I awoke before the 6 a.m. alarm went off and was strongly impressed to get up and read Hebrews 13:5. Like a mantra in my head, "Go read Hebrews 13:5. Go read Hebrews 13:5." Not being a morning person, I hit the snooze alarm again and tried to go back to sleep, but I just kept hearing that nagging message in my spirit. I lay there for a while wondering if Hebrews even had 13 chapters! Finally, I got up and grabbed my NIV Bible and looked up the verse, which reads in part: "Never will I leave you; never will I forsake you."

This phrase leapt off the page at me. I sat and wept. Only God and God alone (until now, of course) knew about my lifelong inner struggle with trust issues, which has kept me from moving forward in my relationship with Him. I couldn't finish this testimony until God gave me the rest of what He wanted me to share with you. Never will He leave you. Never will He forsake you. God's love never ever fails!

Often we feel like we don't deserve to approach God, and we don't on our own merits. Is your relationship with Him what you want it to be? If not, ask for His help, and you can trust that He will gladly give it. His Word instructs us to "come boldly to the throne of grace, that we may obtain mercy and find grace to help in time of need" (Hebrews 4:16 NKJV). God has known us since before we were born; He knows we are not perfect. His ways are better than our ways, and He has our best interests at heart—always! II Samuel 14:14 says that God continually devises ways to bring His people back to Him. Does this sound like a God that gives up easily? A champion is one who defends, fights for a cause, and is victorious. Our God is not a God who gives up on us, not ever! His "cause" is that He loves us. If God is for us, who can be against us?[2]

I could fill volumes with stories of the many mercies God has granted me, but instead, I will leave you with an old hymn that has been meaningful to me this past year. The words to "There's a Wideness in God's Mercy" were written in 1854 by Frederick Faber.

There's a wideness in God's mercy,
Like the wideness of the sea;
There's a kindness in God's justice,
Which is more than liberty.

There is welcome for the sinner,
And more graces for the good;
There is mercy with the Savior;
There is healing in His blood.

For the love of God is broader
Than the measures of man's mind;
And the heart of the Eternal
Is most wonderfully kind.

If our love were but more simple,
We would take Him at his word,
And our lives would be illumined
By the presence of our Lord.

I prayed to the LORD, and he answered me. He freed me from all my fears. Those who look to him for help will be radiant with joy; no shadow of shame will darken their faces (Psalm 34:4-5).

Chapter 8

Passing on the Inheritance

Linda Seaman[1]

Listen, O Israel! The LORD is our God, the LORD alone. And you must love the LORD your God with all your heart, all your soul, and all your strength. And you must commit yourself wholeheartedly to these commands that I am giving you today. Repeat them again and again to your children (Deuteronomy 6:4-6).

My husband and I served for twenty-seven years as church-planting missionaries and had the incredible joy of being eyewitnesses to the spiritual births of many first generation Christians. We quickly came to understand that the difference Christ made in their hearts, lives, homes, and families was so drastic and so hugely impacted their children that most of them came to Christ from sheer longing to know this Jesus who had turned their home right-side up!

Then the Lord brought us back "home" to serve in the "mature" church, and I can't help but wonder if the story, the passion, the individual and family transformation—

this inheritance of ours—hasn't been diluted or taken for granted or even discarded as it has been passed down through the generations. Could it be that because we and our children were born into Christian homes we got the idea we were "right side-up" to begin with?

We have four awesome step-grandsons who were 6, 8, 11, and 13 when they joined our family, but 14 months ago, our first grand baby arrived. Carson was born with Down syndrome; what a gift he has been to our family! Lots of people talk about children like Carson being angels the Lord has graced us with, and my own daughter said when he was a baby, that he might be the only child besides Jesus born without sin! Well, her husband serves as a youth pastor, and they had a senior high retreat two weekends ago, so they asked me to babysit Carson! Last February Carson had pneumonia and coughed quite a bit, and he evidently learned that people paid attention to him when he coughed. It has since become his preferred choice of communication. The first night, I made the mistake of putting him in his high chair before I warmed up his supper, and in a minute or two, he started coughing to let me know the food was not coming fast enough. Before I was able to get back with the mushed up pasta primavera (and I use that term loosely!), his face was beet red, and he sounded like he had TB! Then after I started feeding him, he evidently felt the spoon was not getting back to his mouth quickly enough, so he'd furrow his brow, cough, and slap his little hand twice on the tray. Nope! Nobody's born a Christian! A rich spiritual heritage? Oh, yes! In truth, however, the inheritance cannot be passed on if it is not first received.

I remember clearly the day the familiar passage of scripture in Deuteronomy 6:1-9 leapt off the page and pierced my heart with God's command. Until then, I think I almost thought of my children as a spiritual hindrance to me personally! Gone were the days when time was my own. They demanded so much time and energy; it seemed like they always needed something—day in, day out, night in, night out; they even interrupted my devotions!

In fact, one day I was so aggravated with them when they came bursting through my closed bedroom door while I was on my knees, crying out to God for help! I gave them the "look," and they crept out and shut the door, and I just said, "Oh, Lord, these kids! I can't wait until I'm old, and I can spend all the time I want with You without their interrupting." And He inquired, "When do you think you need to spend more time with me—when you're old or while you are raising them?" Well, He had a point there!

Oh, please understand; I knew exactly how to raise children—before I had any! Thankfully, I was blessed to grow up in a wonderful Christian home. My dad was five when his parents divorced, so his life's goal, often stated, was to raise his three children to love and serve God with, as he used to always pray, a whole heart. Those weren't just words for him either. After he got out of the Marines at the end of World War II, he was accepted at the Illinois Institute of Technology to study engineering. He had a great job opportunity before him because the government had just committed to building the highway system that now crisscrosses our country. He soon realized, however, that the job would require much traveling and time away from his family, so he dropped out and took a factory job instead. I remember when I was ten, the company in Chicago he was working for at the time wanted to promote him and move him to a small town about a hundred miles away. He went to check things out, not the neighborhood or even the schools,

77

only the church to make sure that was where God wanted our family.

I grew up hearing both my parents pray for us, my dad in the early morning hours before he went to work and Mom after lunch every day. We also had family altar when my brothers and I prayed every night, and my parents took turns. That was hard because most of the time we were not exactly on praying ground! Dad later said he could always tell how we were doing spiritually by how we prayed during family altar. I will honestly tell you that we were not cooperative and didn't like it much. We always hoped they would get distracted reading the paper or something and forget, but they never forgot. In the summer, they were a little looser and would let us play outside for a while after we ate supper, but if we didn't come back soon enough, they would get a quick response when they blew the boat horn. We didn't have a boat, mind you, but we did have the horn to call us to prayer!

When I went to college, Dad would send postcards that said, "Keep on your knees! Love, Dad." When my younger brother and his wife backed out of the driveway to head for seminary, as my brother and his wife and my husband and I had done before him, my Dad said that he felt his life's work had been completed.

I wonder how many of us could say that we consider raising our children to love and serve God as our life's work. If someone took a survey, would our goals, dreams and focus for our children and their future be any different than our unchurched neighbors?

My parents weren't perfect. In fact, lots of people were sure we three kids would rebel because they had been so strict, but we didn't. I think in great part it was because they didn't just have rules, regulations, and decrees; they both loved Jesus with all of their heart. They weren't one thing at church and another at home. Their lives were permeated with the Holy Spirit, and while we were far from perfect children, when it came time for each of us to choose, it was an easy decision because what we saw demonstrated in their lives every day was exactly what we wanted! My third generation Christian parents beautifully handed my inheritance to me, and I received it on my own. Gertrude Taylor, one of my spiritual mentors, said, "You are not responsible for your children's choices, but you are responsible for your influence."

My situation was different though, I thought. John and I were called to be missionaries. Unlike my stay-at-home mom and my dad who worked at a secular job, we were working for Jesus. We weren't working to make money; we were working to lead people to the Lord, to accept their inheritance—so we just knew God would help compensate for the sacrifices our kids would have to make.

During our first ten years, we suffered for Jesus on the gorgeous French island of Martinique in the Caribbean, which had to have been the greatest missionary assignment ever! The Lord knew me so well and needed to ease me into missions!

After ten great years, the Lord sent us to West Africa. We went from an island fifty miles long and twenty miles wide to an area of responsibility half a million square miles larger than the United States—from a state of France that enjoyed a rich culture and history, a 99% literacy rate, and the strong influence of the Catholic church to a land ravaged by civil war, malaria, and HIV/AIDS, a part of the world where Islam predated Christianity by a thousand years. We were absolutely sure of our call to West Africa even though we knew it meant John would have to be gone most of the time.

Honestly, I had no idea when we responded so eagerly to this great challenge what it would really mean, what it would cost us. It became obvious immediately that I was going to have to be dependent on God in ways I never had to be before. Not only was the love of my life, my partner in ministry, and wonderful father to our children rarely around, but I also didn't have any friends. I didn't have a church, didn't understand African French very well, and most of the women only spoke their local dialects anyway. I couldn't phone home because I didn't even have a phone. It was just Jesus and me and three kids who were in the throes of their own adjustments.

So it was that the Lord found me complaining on my knees that day and made an attitude correction. Soon I found myself reading the familiar words of Deuteronomy when His command wrapped itself around my heart and gave it a good squeeze. "These commandments that I give you today are to be upon your hearts. Impress them on your children. Talk about them when you sit at home and when you walk along the road, when you lie down and when you get up. Tie them as symbols on your hands and bind them on your foreheads. Write them on the door frames of your houses and on your gates" (Deuteronomy 6:6-8 NIV).

Since I didn't have any books and no Focus on the Family radio programs to help me, I was so desperate! All I had was God's Word and the Lord, and it ended up that was all I really needed anyway! I sense sometimes that the enemy has seduced us into thinking that God's Word is too difficult to understand, that we must always read it through the eyes of another's interpretation.

Jesus told us in John 14:26 that the Father was sending the Holy Spirit to teach us all things and that He would remind us of everything Jesus said. Be bold enough to take God at His Word! There is nothing more exciting than to have God's living Word speak to us through the power and guidance of the Holy Spirit into the very specific need of our heart at any given moment. I don't know that I actually understood all of that; I just knew I didn't have anybody else, so I went to Him and asked Him how in the world I was supposed to do this and what did it even mean exactly.

My life in Africa was so radically different than the one that I had lived in small town USA that the pattern didn't seem to fit. He began to teach me with such compassion, mercy and grace. I had to keep my own relationship with Him fresh and vibrant and growing, and that wasn't hard since I knew I wouldn't be able to survive any other way—let alone have a spiritual inheritance left to hand to my children.

God began to teach me about the talking part. We have often heard that our message to our children is "caught, not taught," but it is clear from this passage that it is both! The Lord drew my attention to the fact that I needed to take every opportunity available to bring Jesus into the conversation as a natural part of our lives together. One of our favorite passages was Philippians 4:6 from the Living Bible, "Don't worry about anything! Pray about everything," and we did! The Lord helped me to become aware of teaching moments, and He taught me all along the way!

One hot day as I was sitting on my bed in late afternoon trying to catch my breath, my oldest came and sat with me, chattering on about things that were not important in my opinion. I was hot, tired, and sweaty, and I really wished she would just go talk to somebody else. At that moment the Lord whispered to my heart, "If you don't pay attention now, when she is a teen and does have something you want to know, she won't come to you."

That little lesson led me later to run to the chair in my bedroom every day, especially when they came home from junior high and high school. I found that when they saw me in my office working at the computer, they would just say "hi" and go to their rooms; however, when I was sitting in my chair reading, they would flop down on the bed and start talking. I told the Lord my kids would grow up thinking I sat in a chair all day, but He said that didn't matter; some day they would figure it out. Even when my youngest was a senior in high school, she would come and sit on my lap if she had a bad day, and it would all come pouring out. It was a critical lesson that became a habit when they were little and made all the difference in our communication as they grew older.

Morning is a wonderful time to pray with your children before they head off to school. I am not a morning person so I totally understand and remember what a hectic time that is. Ask God to help you figure out how to make time, and you will discover how creative He can be!

Bedtime is a precious moment; don't let it become a battlefield. If you put them to bed and read or tell them a story, then let them talk; they will do a lot of talking because they don't want to go to sleep—so just start earlier. I know you are exhausted at the end of a long and demanding day, but you only have so much time; you'll be paying their college bills in a heartbeat, and you are not alone in this. Almighty God, the Maker and Creator of the universe is on your side because you are obediently responding to his command. You will be surprised how He can settle them down. That time with your children before they fall asleep, asking them what prayer request they have and then praying for them individually, is a habit that can continue through their teen years if you are patient and perseverant enough. While I'm sure they did things while they were teens that I will never know about, it is harder for them to live a double life when you pray with them before they go to sleep. Sometimes those moments will be short and uneventful, but, oh, sometimes they will be crucial and life-changing like our own conversations with God.

A Bible story that has impacted me greatly comes from the life of Joshua. God had rescued the Israelites from slavery in Egypt just as He rescues us from our bondage of sin. Then they wandered in the desert for forty years battling back and forth between obedience and disobedience, which is exactly what new Christians experience—battling with their carnal nature, until God through Joshua led them into the Promised Land. For us this is the place that God through our Joshua, Jesus Christ, leads us—to the life of the pure heart filled with the Holy Spirit, our intended inheritance! After the whole nation crossed the Jordan into the Promised Land, the Lord told Joshua to choose twelve men, one from each tribe, to take twelve stones from the middle of the Jordan and place them on the ground as an altar or memorial. That day the Lord used the words, "In the future, when your children ask you, 'What do these stones mean?' tell them...." (Joshua 4:21 NIV) I realized we needed to begin doing this as a family—building our stone altars to serve as a reminder of what God had done in our individual lives and in the life of our family.

I was asked to speak about missions in an old downtown church in Pennsylvania, and the pastor took me over to see the church late Saturday night. It was beautiful, and my attention immediately was drawn to the tall, arched stained-glass windows where, nestled in the deep sills, large jars were filled with white stones. When I asked the pastor to tell me their story, he recounted that when he came as pastor, the church began using these stones to represent answers to prayer from the model in Joshua chapter four.

I began to weep at this beautiful, silent testimony to what God had done in their midst! A simple glass bowl sat on the communion table with a basket of smaller stones sitting next to it. Sunday morning, as the people entered, I noticed many of them came up and placed a stone or two in the glass bowl representing their answers to prayer that week. I think that it would be a wonderful idea for every church and every home. Glass containers and stones are used everywhere now for decorating, and this gives a perfect opportunity for us to use them for spiritual purposes as well.

Here are a few stones that tell a story for the Seaman family.

• The time when John was abducted with a gun held to his head three times—only one of the innumerable times his life was in grave danger—and God brought him back to us safe and unharmed!

• When our older daughter was severely brain-injured in an automobile accident after her first year in college, and doctors said she wouldn't live long enough for us to make it home to say good-bye—but she did. She went on to graduate from college and is now married and a wonderful mother to her four step-sons.

• We had three evacuations during the civil war that broke out in the country we loved, and we were re-assigned to a place eleven time zones away—but God intervened and brought us back home.

• All three of our kids met, fell in love with, and married wonderful Christians, and now our whole family lives in the same time zone. Who would have ever believed God would have done that!

• Carson was born a month early, two days after our daughter and her husband arrived at their pastoral assignment, and we were confused, scared, and didn't understand. Then on the way home from the hospital on that dark and stormy night, the Lord whispered to my heart, "It's just that you don't know Carson yet, but I have been knitting him together in his mother's womb all these days and weeks and months, and when you know him like I know him, you will love him fiercely!" Do we ever!

Is it any wonder the Seaman family loves God and has chosen to follow Him after all He has done for us from generation to generation?

All of us in this place are here because we hunger after a holy heart. We want all that God has for us. We want to be filled with His Holy Spirit so that it flows out of our lives into the lives of those around us. That Deuteronomy 6:4-9 passage applies to all of us whether we have children or not, and we all need stone altars in our lives to remind us of what God has done, of His great faithfulness, and of His love, mercy, and grace. So, when your children ask you, when anyone asks you, be ready to tell them.

We will not hide these truths from our children; we will tell the next generation about the glorious deeds of the LORD, about his power and his mighty wonders....so the next generation might know them—even the children not yet born—and they in turn will teach their own children. So each generation should set its hope anew on God, not forgetting his glorious miracles and obeying his commands (Psalm 78:4, 6-7).

Boot Connections

CTTF Attendees

Boot Surprises

In 2008, a friend invited me to a Come to the Fire conference. I knew Jesus had something special for me so I agreed to go. The moment I entered the room, God met me. I had never told anyone until that day that I could not forgive myself for the choices I had made in my past. The healing began at that conference, and it was life-changing for me. I began to understand that the world without Jesus can be so painful, but Jesus comforts us in the midst of our pain.

I was so thankful to be able to attend. It was a blessing to be in the presence of so many Christian women, the wonderful music, and speakers. The Holy Spirit was present and working His will in each of us. Since that day, I have been holding His hand for safety, peace, joy, love, and comfort. I learned that He removes our sins as far as the east is from the west and remembers them no more. I never knew I could experience the love and peace that I have now because of surrendering my life to Him and obeying His will for me. I came to understand that I had been a slave to sin. I praise the Lord for making me "squeaky clean."

Come to The Fire was in Tennessee in 2009, and it was too far for me to travel—but not for Jesus! I prayed, and the Lord arranged for me to join nine other beautiful Christian women to drive to Nashville! It was at that conference that I met my new friend and prayer partner. We were both wearing therapeutic boots.

I did not want to wear my boot to Come to the Fire; it was cumbersome and not so pretty, but I obeyed the doctor. Had I not worn it, I probably would not have met my new friend. She noticed me the first night. The next morning, when she saw me sitting on a sofa in the lobby, she came to me showing she had a special shoe like mine. Then she told me that she had seen me the evening before and had been praying for me throughout the night. We sat together that morning and the remainder of the conference. We talked and cried like sisters.

She introduced me to Patsy Lewis who asked me to help with the Saturday prayer time praying in my native tongue of Spanish. At first I told her that I had only prayed in English since becoming a Christian. When she assured me that all I had to say was the opening of the Lord's Prayer, I agreed to do it.

I hobbled to the podium in my boot, and as I began to say in Spanish the introduction to The Lord's Prayer, "Our Father which art in heaven, hallowed be Thy name," I was overwhelmed with the presence of God and became speechless. While I stood there transfixed, soaking in His glory, I felt someone put her arm around me. Beth Coppedge had come from the front row probably thinking I had stage fright and wanting to give me support. My heart was so moved as I prayed in Spanish;

then I realized why Patsy encouraged us to pray in our native language. It was powerful.

Oh, God's love is overwhelming!

Spirit Connections

I learned about Come to the Fire in a phone conversation with Patsy Lewis in August 2008. We discussed the possibility of the church where I work in Grove City, Ohio, hosting the conference in the future. I became a Come to the Fire prayer partner and invited several friends to attend the 2009 conference with me.

Patsy asked me to be an altar worker, and I attended the altar workers' training Thursday afternoon prior to the conference. I was recovering from a broken foot and was wearing a boot and walking with a walker. During the training I remember Patsy telling us to be alert to people around us and to be praying for them. This is what I committed in my heart to do. I had already decided that I would not make my way to the altar to pray with someone because I didn't want to cause a disturbance and break a reverent atmosphere by clunking my way down the aisle.

That evening I tried to be aware of any ladies around me that I felt the Lord might be directing me to pray for but felt no specific leadings. After the altar call, as ladies were returning to their seats, I saw a dark-haired lady coming up the aisle toward me. She had been weeping and looked as though she was still burdened. I thought, "Lord, is she the one?" and I began to pray for her. I tried to see where she sat without being too obvious. I found that she was sitting directly behind me, and I told the Lord I would talk with her after the service. At the conclusion of the service, I gathered my belongings and set up my walker. By the time I looked up, she was heading toward the door, and I lost her in the crowd. I thought, "I was willing, but she disappeared, so she must not be the one." However, that night I couldn't get her out of my mind.

The next morning I awakened thinking about her. I told the Lord if he wanted me to talk with her, He would have to bring us together in that sea of ladies. When we arrived at the church, I immediately saw her sitting by herself just outside the Worship Center. I was surprised to see she was wearing a boot—just like mine! I hadn't noticed it the night before. She looked up and saw me, and I pointed to my boot. I asked if I could join her, and we began to talk about our injuries. Then I told her I had been praying for her since the previous evening and asked if there was something specific I could pray for her. We spent at least a half hour together, talking and praying. We traded prayer requests and contact information and promised to stay in touch—and we have.

Come to the Fire was different from any conference or retreat I have attended. I heard the term "holy heart" used over and over. I said, "Lord, that's what I want—a holy heart."

God is teaching me that having a holy heart is not a goal to attain, but a daily love relationship with Him. For many years I have been telling God I want a deeper walk with Him. This conference was the next step in my journey. The music, the testimonies, and the speakers all led me into a personal worship experience and a time of heart searching. The message of the conference for me was encouragement and admonition to continue to develop a daily, moment-by-moment dependence on and obedience to God, the Holy Spirit. I also learned that "altar work" is a heart condition and a call to be ready at anytime, anywhere to see a need and be willing to pray for that need.

Part V

Reflect His Glory

Aletha Hinthorn

Then the nations will know that I am the LORD, declares the Sovereign LORD when I show myself holy through you before their eyes (Ezekiel 36:23 NIV).

To reflect God's glory is our most awesome privilege. God wants the world to see the beauty of His holiness in us. God is love, so His holiness in us will look like love— not a self-serving love—but God's selfless love. As we draw from Him moment by moment, others see God's glory.

"But whenever someone turns to the Lord, the veil is taken away, for the Lord is the Spirit, and wherever the Spirit of the Lord is, there is freedom. So all of us who have had that veil removed can see and reflect the glory of the Lord. And the Lord—who is the Spirit—makes us more and more like him as we are changed into his glorious image" (2 Corinthians 3:16-18).

Chapter 9

Campus Prayer Adventures

Patsy Lewis

Now all glory to God, who is able, through his mighty power at work within us, to accomplish infinitely more than we might ask or think (Ephesians 3:20).

Come to the Fire 2010 was held at the performing arts auditorium of the University of Indiana-Purdue Ft. Wayne Campus. Each year I arrange my schedule to arrive early so I can pray and read Scripture in and around the building where the conference will be held. Often I have opportunities to meet with local CTTF committees and community leaders.

I arrived in Ft. Wayne on Monday and attended a final meeting of the CTTF committee chairpersons that night. Our prayer time was rich, and I knew these ladies had devoted untold hours to prayer and planning. Before going to bed, I received a message from the overseer of the Christian organizations on campus telling me of an early prayer time Tuesday morning that I was welcome to attend. I had some difficulty finding the location of the prayer group and entered the room discretely since the university students were already lifting prayers. Their prayers immediately touched me. I don't think anyone even glanced up when I entered because they were praying so intently.

Two young men prayed as I had never heard before—passionately filling their prayers with praise interlaced with Scripture—fluent, transparent, and sincere. At the close of the session, one of them asked me to share how they could pray for me which gave me the opportunity to tell them about Come to the Fire and two Christian gatherings on campus where I had been asked to speak Tuesday and Wednesday evenings. This band of students then prayed fervently for me led by the young man who had inquired about how they could pray for me. One sentence continues to echo, and I've prayed it often for myself and others: "May she lay down and take up according to Your purposes!" I made plans to meet them again for prayer the next two mornings.

In conversation before we parted, one of the young women told how she had been to a retreat the weekend before and had been praying for the fire of God's presence to sweep across their campus. As she was walking across campus when she returned, she noticed a small flame drawn on a building and wondered if we were responsible when she heard me say, "Come to the Fire." She felt sure her prayers and our presence on this university campus were related, and she told me she would be at the meeting where I was speaking that night.

I made additional God ordained connections that Tuesday night at a Christian student gathering. One upperclassman told me I delivered a message that was meant specifically for him. I used a phrase in one example that I don't recall ever using before, and he said that phrase precisely defined where he was in his spiritual journey. The friend I had made at the early morning prayer meeting introduced me to her roommate, and I made new acquaintances reminding me that when I go to a location for Come to the Fire, I am there for much more than a conference.

Wednesday night's group was a totally different student organization, building location, and format from the Tuesday night meeting, but even in the unfamiliarity, God empowered me to proclaim the message He had placed in my heart.

The next day one student visited the CTTF book tables as they were being set up, purchased a book, and talked with Dr. Daniel Hinthorn saying he had heard a lady speak the night before and out of curiosity came to explore. Dr. Hinthorn and a group of doctors in Kansas had been praying for weeks that male students would be impacted by CTTF in Indiana.

At the second morning prayer meeting, Gloria, a student from the continent of Africa, captured my heart with her prayers and love of Jesus. I asked her if she could attend Come to the Fire Thursday night and pray in both her language and English. She timidly hesitated and even protested that she wasn't sure she could do it until others encouraged her that she could and should accept. She wondered if anyone would be there who would understand her language, and I shared with her that although I did not know, we wanted women to be assured that all cultures are warmly received and to be comfortable praying in their native tongue.

When she arrived at the service Thursday evening, she had a friend with her, also a student from Africa. My daughter, Lanissa, was sitting with us, and dear friends of hers had just arrived in Togo as missionaries. Gloria's friend was from a country bordering Togo, and she and Lanissa had a lively conversation as they sat together.

Gloria was on the university newspaper staff and brought the latest issue for me to see the headlines of an article that troubled her. She asked me to pray for her as she was trying to shine the light of Jesus while meeting some resistance from those of differing views. As I stood beside her on the platform and heard her anointed prayer in both languages, I could sense the Spirit had carried her words into the heavenly realms. To her surprise, a young lady from the conference ran to her following the service enthusiastically speaking to Gloria in her African language. Jenny had recently returned from Gloria's area of Africa on a ministry trip rescuing girls from sex trafficking. After we said good-bye to Jenny, Gloria looked up into the balcony and spotted one of her professors, which opened a door for future communication about the Lord.

On Thursday, following the early morning prayer session, I prayer walked with a campus ministry leader. To conclude our walk, I took her to see the prayer rooms that were being set up. These were actually three voice and piano practice rooms at the end of a long corridor of similar practice rooms. I told her to spread the word that students were invited to visit those prayer rooms that were clearly marked. Later she reported to me that students had accepted the invitation to find a quiet place of prayer.

At the close of the conference, the student praying for fire to spread on her campus was waiting for me at my book table. She said, "I couldn't let you leave without telling you good-bye!" Then she continued, "I've been crying all morning in the session, and when I knelt to pray, a lady came beside me and prayed silently at first. Later she prayed words of blessing over me."

At that moment, a dear prayer partner from New York City walked up to tell me good-bye, and the student exclaimed, "Oh, there she is! The lady who prayed with me!" We continued to communicate when she prepared to go on a mission trip the next year and when she returned. Also, the campus ministry leader that joined me to prayer walk has kept contact from time to time. Yes, Come to the Fire is an on-going adventure, and we are to reflect His glory wherever He leads. We can be assured we are always there for a greater purpose than we realize.

Glory to him in the church and in Christ Jesus through all generations forever and ever! Amen (Ephesians 3:21).

Chapter 10

I Did Not Want to Go

Ellie Keller

On the Sabbath we went a little way outside the city to a riverbank, where we thought people would be meeting for prayer, and we sat down to speak with some women who had gathered there. One of them was Lydia from Thyatira, a merchant of expensive purple cloth, who worshiped God. As she listened to us, the Lord opened her heart, and she accepted what Paul was saying. She was baptized along with other members of her household, and she asked us to be her guests (Acts 16:13-15).

No! I did not want to go to another retreat that was going to be just like the other 200+ retreats I had already attended in my life! As the wife of a pastor, I had attended more than my share, and in essence they were all the same.

I heard about Come to the Fire in Georgia when I attended a Lydia Prayer Retreat in February 2008. I had been asked to be the global prayer director for my denomination, and a key leader had discovered the retreat while surfing the web. It was a joy to meet at the historic Epworth by the Sea Retreat Center with approximately a hundred women from eighteen states and eleven denominations.

I loved the women I met from the Lydia Prayer Ministry leadership, and the Holy Spirit was very evident during the weekend I was there. I went home with a calling to begin a Lydia Prayer Ministry in my church and eventually in my Michigan District denomination, but when they invited me to attend the next Come to the Fire, I said, "No, thank you," and I did not share anything about it with anyone for two years!

As I flew back to Michigan, the prayer of my heart was to find a Lydia Prayer partner. During the retreat, we had been inspired by speakers and met in small prayer groups, and though we were mostly strangers in one sense, we were sisters in the Lord being drawn together by the Holy Spirit. His presence unified our spirits throughout the weekend, and God was showing me a prayer ministry that could change not only my life, but the lives of women like me—though at the time I was not completely aware of my part in His plan.

My first step was to seek the Lord's personal direction to find another woman who would share my burden and be willing to meet weekly with me for prayer. God answered that prayer in a beautiful way, and Sharyl and I began meeting together by the riverside every Monday morning in May of 2008. My home is in Port Huron, Michigan, which is located on the banks of Lake Huron and the St. Clair River. Reading the story of the Apostle Paul's meeting with Lydia and her prayer group by the riverside was an inspiration we could easily fulfill.

After meeting with Sharyl for a year, I began to ask the Lord to raise up others who would start a Lydia Prayer Ministry. One morning as I was praying about this, I felt the Lord impressing me to be the one to get this started. He had the perfect answer for my question of "How should I do this?" I was to hold brunches in my home and invite ladies to hear my Lydia Prayer story. I invited friends for food and fellowship, then shared my testimony about my trip to St. Simons Island. I told how God had called me to become a Lydia Prayer partner and how God had blessed our prayer time over the past year. From the four breakfasts I held in March and April of 2009, Lydia Prayer groups were started. The news spread, more women asked about the ministry, and now we have twenty Lydia Prayer groups with over fifty women involved.[1]

In the fall of 2009, when a friend from church told me she was invited to Nashville to attend a retreat in November, I was not interested in attending even though she told me the name of the conference was Come to the Fire.

Finally, on a Friday morning in 2010, I was getting ready to teach a small Bible study in my home, and the Lord spoke to me saying, "Ask your friends if they would like to go to Fort Wayne with you for Come to the Fire." My response was, "They won't want to go, but I will ask!"

I started by saying, "You wouldn't want to go to Come to the Fire with me in October, would you?"

Sharyl quickly responded, "Yes! Yes, we would!"

The rest of the story is history! We went. My prayer partner's life was changed, and because of the change in her, our women's ministry sponsored a bus trip in 2011 with seventeen women; in 2012 we had fifty-two women; and in 2013 there were seventy-five plus going by bus and cars! In 2014 it was live streamed at my church, and several drove to Grove City to be on site for the conference. We have all been powerfully changed. In 2015 and 2016 I have been showing videos from past

CTTF conferences to ladies in my Bible study groups; then we dig into the Scripture references used in the messages—so Come to the Fire continues to spread throughout the women of our church.

Was CTTF the same as the other 200+ retreats I had attended? No way! It was an incredible experience where the presence of the Holy Spirit was working in all of our lives because of the prayer covering over every attendee. My life has never been the same since 2008 when I attended the Lydia Prayer Retreat in Georgia, and again in 2010 when I attended Come to the Fire in Fort Wayne —and every time since. You don't want to miss a minute of this powerful and anointed ministry that will change your life! Please, Come to the Fire.

On the last day, the climax of the festival, Jesus stood, and shouted to the crowds, "Anyone who is thirsty may come to me! Anyone who believes in me may come and drink! For the Scriptures declare, 'Rivers of living water will flow from his heart.'" When he said, "living water," he was speaking of the Spirit, who would be given to everyone believing in him (John 7:37-39).

Joyful Fellowship

CTTF Attendees

Partnership

I was sitting at a Bible study with my prayer partner Ellie and another lady. Ellie asked us if we wanted to go to a women's conference called Come To The Fire. I immediately said yes as I'm always ready for a new experience. Listening to other women share is not a new experience for me, but I didn't know how different and life changing Come to the Fire was going to be. I wanted what the speakers were talking about—a closer relationship with Jesus. The atmosphere at the conference was contagious. You could feel that something different and powerful was going on. The Holy Spirit was there.

When we got home, I shared with our church's Women's Steering Committee what I had experienced. The next year the committee organized a busload to go to Come To The Fire. It wasn't until on the bus ride home that they said it was because of the change they saw in me that they wanted to go. I was shocked.

Sometimes when Jesus is working in our life, we are totally unaware of how it can also affect others.

Sisterhood

One of my vivid memories of Come to the Fire was several young moms and their pastor's wife who came as a group and stayed together at a local motel. Their homes were less than an hour's drive from the site of the conference; nevertheless, they thought it best to stay there together for the entire time. Although I had never met these young ladies before, it was my honor and privilege to pray with many of them during the conference. It was a great joy to hear them tell how they had held bakes sales and garage sales all during the year to earn enough money to be able to stay together during the conference. That time together created an awesome bonding, and I was humbled to be able to witness their sense of sisterhood that was fostered by being together for Come to the Fire.

I think also of a busload of ladies who have never yet missed a Come to the Fire conference, traveling each time hundreds of miles to get there. I cannot tell you how excited I am about seeing them again at the next conference. I am expecting the fire to fall just as it has in each of the other Come to the Fire conferences. I praise Him that it is still possible to meet with women from all over the country who yearn to be squeaky clean in this present generation! Come to the Fire! What an appropriate name for the Holy Spirit's cleansing, purifying, and warming of the willing heart both individually and collectively![1]

101

Affirmation

I love Come to the Fire! I would love to round up every woman I know and bring her to the conference! Our God reigns in the purpose and planning of every event. Seeing women from our church who have come to the conference year after year grow in the Lord and their faith has been so affirming that the work is truly of God. I have had the privilege of praying with women at the Come to the Fire Conference. What a huge blessing that has been! So often it felt as though the Lord had hand selected the women that I was blessed to pray with. God brought to my mind memory verses, examples, and encouraging words that I knew came right from Him. He is so kind and faithful! I want to serve HIM forever!

Servanthood

Come to the Fire has impacted me by helping me experience a holy heart and to live by the power of the Holy Spirit. A couple of months before this year's Come to the Fire, God showed me the place He wanted me to serve Him. I felt the anointing of the Holy Spirit this year. I have found my place in the Great Commission through attending Come to the Fire.

Part VI

Enter His Rest

Aletha Hinthorn

The promise of entering his rest still stands (Hebrews 4:1).

God promised to give the Israelites the land of Canaan, a land where they would overcome all their enemies and find complete satisfaction. The writer to the Hebrews compares their entering into Canaan to our entering into our Sabbath rest, which is freedom from the struggle resulting from a divided heart. God calls the end of that struggle a rest. How true! When we are "in Him" we are in Canaan, the land of abundance and rest.

Jesus said: "Come to me, all you who are weary and burdened, and I will give you rest. Take my yoke upon you and learn from me, for I am gentle and humble in heart, and you will find rest for your souls. For my yoke is easy and my burden is light" (Matthew 11:28-30 NIV).

Chapter 11

Passing on a Passion for Jesus Through Worship

Cricket Albertson[1]

O LORD, our Lord, how majestic is your name in all the earth! You have set your glory above the heavens. From the lips of children and infants you have ordained praise... *(Psalm 8:1-2).*

One afternoon, I dropped off my two older children at cross-country practice and pulled out of the parking lot with only my younger son in the back seat. I was distracted, and he was chattering when suddenly he caught my attention. "Mama, do you know my friend, Joshua? Today I asked him if he knew Jesus. He said that he did not, so I asked him if he wanted to ask Jesus into his heart."

Quickly, I gave my son my full attention and asked, "What did he say?"

"Mom, he said he did want to ask Jesus into his heart. So, right there in computer class, I told him to repeat after me. And he prayed, 'Jesus, would You come into my heart?"

We celebrated together in the car, and he continued to talk, "Mama, I have a dream. In it there are cars going to heaven, and the rule is that only one person can go in each car. But Mama, I am going to break that rule. I am going to fill up the back of my car with my friends. You are going to sit in the driver's seat, and I am going to sit next to you." With his little hand he motioned behind him, "And we are going to fill up our car!" He paused for a moment and then said, "Mama, I already have two!"

As I listened to this little one share his faith in Jesus, I found my heart worshipping. Both of us were lost in worship in that car; my son was exalting in his obedience and God's faithfulness, and I was in awe of God's ways with our children. When I was asked to share my testimony at Come to the Fire in 2011, particularly about passing on a passion for Jesus to the next generation, one word kept coming to my mind—worship! That day in the car with my son, we were both filled with worship. Passing on a passion for Jesus from parent to child or from child to parent begins in worship. As we worship the living Lord Jesus, we invite our children and others to worship as well.

The Holy Spirit has used Matthew 2 to lead me into His presence; it is the first story of worship in the New Testament, the first account of someone falling down at the feet of the Lord Jesus. Matthew 2 is the story of the wise men, and I want their story to be the frame for my story.

Jesus was born in the town of Bethlehem in Judea, during the reign of King Herod. About that time some wise men from eastern lands arrived in Jerusalem asking, "Where is the newborn king of the Jews? We have seen his star as it arose, and we have come to worship him....after this interview the wise men went on their way. Once again, the star appeared to them, guiding them to Bethlehem. It went ahead of them and stopped over the place where the child was. When they saw the star, they were filled with joy! They entered the house where the child and his mother, Mary, were, and they fell down before him and worshipped him. Then they opened their treasure chests and gave him gifts of gold, frankincense and myrrh. But when it was time to leave, they went home another way, because God had warned them in a dream not to return to Herod" (Matthew 2:1-2, 9-11).

I love that the wise men came to Jesus as they were. These men were not Jews; they belonged to the religious caste among the Persians. Traditionally, magi were devoted to astrology, divination, and interpretation of dreams. They did not become Jews before they came to Jesus. They simply followed His star and came to worship Him with all their foreign nature and strangeness; yet, when they left his small home in Bethlehem, they were followers of the King of kings. Jesus has been inviting me to come to Him just as I am and worship. I come to Him in my brokenness, and He heals and frees and redeems!

Let me give you a little background to my love story with Jesus. When I was thirteen years old, one autumn day after an argument with my mother, I ran down the street in adolescent agony of soul. I was desperate for God to do something deeper for me. In anger and frustration, I cried out to Him, "If You can't do something for me, I can't keep pretending. I give You three years to work a change in my heart and in my nature. If in three years, You have not done something for me, I think I am done with You."

On that day, I began to know the passionate pursuing nature of God. I began to prove Him. I had given him space and time to work in my life, and now I felt it was up to Him to show Himself mighty to save and transform me. The next three years provided some of the most painful moments of my life to that point, but as I navigated my way through those pains, I found He never left me. He came to meet me at every turn, and He provided blessing after blessing. Three years later on the night of that anniversary, I found myself in a small bedroom in Paris. I was talking to Jesus before I went to sleep, when I was reminded of the date. I knelt beside my little air mattress on the floor in that bedroom with my sister asleep next to me, and I worshipped. I knew that He was mine, and I was His forever!

Over the next twenty years, He worked in my heart, and my desire was for Him. I married my high school sweetheart and best friend, attended Seminary, worked with my grandfather doing devotional and theological work, and had three beautiful children. Things seemed perfect, but then, I found myself facing emergency after emergency and disappointment after disappointment. Systematically and deliberately, it seemed that my foundations were being rattled.

The Holy Spirit peeled away the layers of defense that I had carefully built around my soul until my heart felt naked before him in pride and insecurity and fear. He began to point to specific things and ask, "Do you trust me here?" I did not know how to answer Him because I felt unsure. After a year of stress and unsettling situations, I found myself deeply afraid. In my fear, I panicked. If, after having loved Jesus for twenty years, so much fear still lived inside of me, I began to doubt the power of God to bring transformation and change in a human heart. My fear turned to panic and the panic to doubt, and like Eve I began to question the goodness of God. One day, sitting at my kitchen table, overwhelmed by a fear I could not name, I cried out to him to rescue me. He heard my cry!

He came to me in my distress, and He asked me to worship! He asked me to come to him in my pride and with my fears and kneel at his feet and worship. Somehow, I had been trying to handle life in my own strength, and my mind and heart and memory needed a deeper healing and sanctifying touch. My wounded places needed the hands of the Holy One to make me whole. Instead of trying to get myself free from fear or insecurity, He invited me to come to Him in the midst of it. "Come to me as you are and worship me!"

I have found that in worship, the attention is on Jesus and not on me, and the Holy Spirit has room to come in and clean house. In worship, I am free to confess my inadequacy and His enoughness. In worship, I kneel before Him in weakness, and He comes to me in His strength and gives me rest.

When the wise men came to worship Jesus, they found Him! The star led the wise men straight to the place where Jesus was. They stopped to ask Herod, but it was God's star that led them all the way to the place where Jesus was with his mother. God promises that He will be found by those who seek. He wants to be found by us. In fact, He is coming to meet us every moment of every day if we have ears to hear his voice. God the Father was willing to change the course of the stars in the heavens so that the wise men could find Him. Whatever distance the wise men traveled to worship, the Son of God came an infinitely farther distance to meet them. They had come from the east, He from outside time and space. They had spent months following his star; His coming had been planned from the beginning of time. Whatever price they had paid to worship in time, money, and risk, He had paid the highest price by emptying himself and taking on the form of a servant, willingly humbling himself enough to take on flesh.

Is God good? Will He come to meet us? The testimony of the wise men and of my own heart is YES! A thousand times YES! He will pay any price to prove this to us. As the Holy Spirit led me on a journey of worship step by step through each fear and wounded place, He revealed His willingness to exchange my hurt for His love. He would whisper to my heart, "Invite me here into this place, and I will come."

I have had the joy of watching Him come. I am learning to invite Him in to every moment and every relationship and every activity. As I wait on Him in worship, I find joy and strength in His presence.

When the wise men worshipped Jesus, they represented all nations and all peoples. The first picture we have of worship in the New Testament includes the whole world, and it fulfills the promise of God in the Old Testament.

"Kings will see you...princes will see you and bow down, because of the LORD who is faithful, the Holy One of Israel, who has chosen you....Kings will be your foster fathers, and their queens your nursing mothers. They will bow down before you with their faces to the ground....Then you will know that I am the LORD; those who hope in me will not be disappointed" (Isaiah 49:7, 23 NIV).

This picture of worship gives us a promise of what God is going to do. We have the joy and privilege of participating in this fulfillment of His good intentions every time we worship Jesus. The first worship scene in the New Testament is the fulfillment of Old Testament prophecy, and it points the way to the end of all human history when kings will bow down before Him and offer their treasures. When we worship Jesus, as individuals or families or churches, we participate in God's eternal purpose for the world. A day is coming when every knee will bow, and creation itself will proclaim the Lordship of Jesus Christ to the glory of the Father. Worship transforms the mundane tasks of our days into moments when time and eternity join together in joy.

Passionate love for Jesus is passed from one generation to the next—not in formulas or religious behavior or even in service. When mothers and fathers have a passion in their hearts to know Jesus and be known by Him, then an invitation is given to their children, school children, and the neighbor children to enter into worship as well. When we love Jesus with all our hearts and receive His love for us, it makes it possible for others to know the goodness of God's love and the salvation that only knowing Jesus brings. One of the joys of my life has been to watch Christ come into our home, calling and speaking to our children. As we invite Him to come and give Him time and space to speak, He comes and speaks and calls. Our children, then, have the opportunity to respond to Him.

One day, we will all gather around His throne, and the language that will bind us all together will be the language of worship.

"After these things, I heard a loud voice of a great multitude in heaven saying, 'Alleluia! Salvation and glory and honor and power belong to the Lord our God! For true and righteous are His judgments'....Again, they said, 'Alleluia!'...And the twenty-four elders and the four living creatures fell down and worshiped God who sat on the throne, saying 'Amen! Alleluia!' Then a voice came from the throne, saying, 'Praise our God, all you His servants and those who fear Him, both small and great!' And I heard, as it were, the voice of a great multitude, as the sound of many waters and as the sound of mighty thunderings, saying 'Alleluia!' for the Lord God Omnipotent reigns! Let us be glad and rejoice and give him the glory!" (Revelation 19:1-7 NKJV).

Chapter 12

Rest Stops

Patsy Lewis

So we praise God for the glorious grace he has poured out on us who belong to his dear Son. He is so rich in kindness and grace that he purchased our freedom with the blood of his Son and forgave our sins (Ephesians 1:6-7).

My daughter, Lanissa, our friend Yori, and I were sitting on the front row at Come to the Fire 2011 during Aletha Hinthorn's Friday morning message about the blood of Jesus. As a scarlet chiffon canopy was draped across the front of Grove City Church of the Nazarene's sanctuary, Aletha concluded with these words: "If you believe that Jesus's blood will meet your need of forgiveness or cleansing, we're inviting you to get up out of your seat and pass under this cloth that symbolizes the blood of Jesus that was over the doorposts and saved the Israelites. You may want to kneel at the altar or go back to your seat. Jesus will meet you. Let us honor the blood."

As Lanissa and I stood together under the crimson canopy, we were deeply touched and reminded that the blood of Jesus had covered our sins, cleansed our hearts, and purified us as finest gold. We were aware of His glorious presence, willing for Him to continue to refine us, and eager to enter His rest.

As an eight year old, Lanissa had been baptized by her father when he pastored at Grove City Church of the Nazarene. She and I both had experienced God's amazing grace and love through the years since her baptism, and at every Come to the Fire, He took us deeper into our relationship with Him and each other.

As I approached the platform to lead a prayer session after this moving experience, I noticed my friend Yori sitting on the front row with a radiant face. In a spontaneous moment, I began to tell Yori's story and how it had affected Lanissa and me.

Yori was a successful dancer and actor in France when she met her Prince Charming who was truly a prince, but as soon as he learned she was "with child," he fled the relationship. Yori later married an English lord, and when that marriage dissolved, she married a famous French actor and gave birth to a son. In spite of the glamorous life she led, she was insecure, lonely, and unhappy. Her third marriage was to an extremely wealthy man. She traveled in private jets, had a chauffeur, and purchased anything money could buy; however, royalty, riches, and fame did not bring fulfillment and peace. At one point she had a personal fortune teller traveling with her around the world. She became involved in all sorts of occult practices only to become more and more anxious and depressed. Suicide became an obsession. She left her billionaire husband, took her son, and moved to America leaving her adult daughter in France. Pills, panic attacks, and hallucinations were now a way of life for her, and the pain was excruciating.

Alone in America with her son, no money, and filled with trauma, Yori met a neighbor who seemed to have consistent joy and peace; this intrigued Yori. Betty genuinely cared for Yori and shared the love of Jesus. Yori began to read the Bible and asked God to reveal truth to her. She accepted this truth and became a believer in Christ. When she found the verse in the Bible which said, "Therefore, if anyone is in Christ, he is a new creation. The old has passed away; behold, the new has come" (II Corinthians 5:17 ESV), she realized she was that new creation. Jesus totally turned her life around. Yori learned there is hope for the broken heart and restless soul. She accepted the invitation to enter His rest.

When Yori returned to France to visit her daughter, Eve saw that her mother was a new creation and inquired about the change saying, "You are not the same person. This is the first time I've seen you happy. What has happened? Do you have a new man in your life?"

Yori began to tell Eve about Jesus, and this was Eve's response: "She began to talk about Jesus and what He had done for us. It was like an evidence for me. It was so real. I didn't know anything about Jesus. I just knew that what she had, I wanted it. I was twenty-four years old and looked fine on the outside, but there was not one day I did not think about killing myself. When she talked to me about Jesus, I felt like something was happening at the mention of His name and this was the answer to all my doubts and fears. I had been waiting for something to change in my life, and I knew right away that He was the answer to the questions I had for so long. We talked all night. I cried and cried, but for the first time, my tears were not tears of sorrow but of joy. That very night, I gave my heart to Jesus and felt so loved by Him.[1]

"She asked my forgiveness for all she had done or not done that had wounded me in the past; however, she did not do it in a general way. She asked me to recall and name every hurtful thing so that she could specifically ask for my forgiveness. This was so strong to me because I had always wanted her to acknowledge my suffering and pain—and that she was responsible for this. We covered a lot of ground that night, but the process lasted two years. Each time a hurtful memory would come to mind, I would share with her, and she would ask my forgiveness again. It was a cleansing process. The wall between us crumbled, and there was no longer separation. I felt loved by her and loved by my Father in heaven. I know this was tough on my mother but liberating for both of us. At last, I had a mother, a mother who cared about me and who became my best friend!"[2]

I met Eve in the summer of 2009 when she was in Nashville visiting Yori and I was there for a Come to the Fire council meeting. They told their story to those of us at the lunch table, and I invited Yori and Eve to give this testimony at the Come to the Fire conference that fall. As we parted, I expressed that I was going to speak the same words to my daughter that Yori had said to Eve asking her to tell everything she had done or not done that had hurt her so she could ask forgiveness. That opportunity came within a few days.

It was now Come to the Fire 2011, and I was telling this unrehearsed story of Yori and Eve when I spotted my daughter on the front row. I spontaneously asked her to join me on the platform. I continued the story of how one week after meeting Eve, Lanissa came from Dallas to my home in Oklahoma City for a brunch I was having for my Lydia Prayer group and their daughters. Standing at my kitchen sink the night before the brunch, I told Lanissa about seeing Yori in Nashville and meeting Eve. I relayed the story that you just read, and we talked, prayed, and cried together into the night. Our deep conversations continued throughout the weekend.

Neither Lanissa nor I remember all we said in that unprepared moment Friday morning, but many women came afterward to tell us they were going home to ask their daughter or son Yori's question. Our prayer sessions that year were called Rest Stops, and we closed that service with the prayer that walls would come down and mothers and daughters would truly "Enter His Rest."

Many mothers and daughters attend CTTF together and leave strengthened in their relationship to become a spiritual force in their families, churches, and communities. God is giving women holy hearts and using them to change the world! I continue to pray:

"Jesus, we give you praise for Your amazing work in our hearts and for Your wise counsel and healing touch even in relationships that are closest to our hearts! May every mother and daughter who has attended Come to the Fire, or who reads this story, experience a greater level of intimacy in their relationship as You take them deeper into their love for You and each other."[3]

Those who live in the shelter of the Most High will find rest in the shadow of the almighty (Psalm 91:1).

Hungry Hearts

CTTF Attendees

Hungry for God's Word

I didn't know what to expect when I arrived at Come to the Fire, but the moment I stepped in the church, I felt the presence of God and knew that this assembly had been bathed in months and months of prayer. I understood how God had led me there, and I was right where I needed to be to receive His encouragement for the months ahead. I would recall the messages I had heard, the feeling of freedom to worship, and the images of hundreds of ladies praying and worshiping together time and time again when, over the next year, I would face some tough personal and spiritual battles. Before returning home from CTTF, I purchased the entire DVD set to show the ladies of my church. I made posters, showed clips of the conference on Sunday mornings, prepared, and prayed. The first night we had seventeen ladies attend! Those six weeks led us into a Bible study, then another, and another. Our weekly Bible study continues to have a dedicated group of ladies hungry for the Word of God.[1]

Hungry for Clean Hearts

I became aware of the Lydia Prayer Movement at a Titus Women's Leadership Summit the year before I attended Come to the Fire. Right away I saw the love and joy these ladies had for one another. My heart was noticeably pounding the whole time I was at the Summit. When Linda Boyette spoke, I knew I wanted to go from an "average" Christian to one whose heart was holy and squeaky clean for Jesus! Linda prayed with me, and I have not been the same since.

I went home desiring to start a Lydia Prayer group for ladies and another one for young girls. I had been meeting with my Lydia Prayer groups several months before attending Come to the Fire where I saw a huge number of women with a desire to have a holy, squeaky clean heart in order to live for Jesus and to honor Him! It was amazing to see hundreds of women worshipping the God of all creation with open hearts, hungry for what He has in store for us. He is so deserving of our worship and praise!

The teaching at Come to the Fire was out of this world! The testimonies were priceless! I have learned that we can serve God best when we are full of Him—when we have holy hearts and are lovers of Jesus! This is the inheritance I want to leave my family, my Little Lydias, and all those God places in my life![2]

Hungry for Jesus

I was a pray-er before, but after attending Come to the Fire, I knew God wanted me to be an intercessor through bold prayer, using His promises in Scripture! The conference was so filled with Jesus. Every song and speaker ushered me into His presence. It was a foretaste of heaven! The name of Jesus is on my lips in a new way.

Hungry for the Overflow

During announcements my church was promoting a ladies' conference called Come to the Fire. What was that? It sounded different from any other conference I'd attended, so I decided to go—still not quite sure what it would be like. I figured I'd find out when I got there. Well, I surely did!

The name summed it up for me—going to the fire of God with all my burdens and pain that I had been holding onto for years and leaving it at the altar, being in a worship time with the fire burning inside of me, sensing the presence of God so near that I felt like I could no longer stand and just dropping to my knees. The presence of God was flowing like I had never experienced. During the healing service, the grace of God was overflowing on thousands of women as we repented of sins we'd held onto for years, getting rid of anger, strongholds, and offenses. God's love and mercy was surrounding us, healing us in such a powerful way. I couldn't believe what I was experiencing. Hebrews 12:28-29 became so real to me: "Therefore, since we are receiving a kingdom that cannot be shaken, let us hold onto grace. By it, we may serve God acceptably with reverence and awe, for our God is a consuming fire." (HCSB)

Hungry for a Deeper Connection

I had been to so many women's conferences over the years, but nothing like this. My husband was texting and calling me throughout the first day of the conference, but there came a point on day two that I kindly had to ask

119

him not to text or call because I didn't want any interruptions during this amazing encounter I was having with God. It was sacred! I had been longing for this for so many years, and it was finally happening.

I went down for the altar call where each lady was anointed with oil if she wanted and an altar worker prayed for any need she had. Then we could pick a verse just for us from a box. We also wrote any sin or struggle on an index card and left it up front to be prayed over by the conference leaders. By the time I left the altar, I was so filled with the Spirit of God and so renewed that I actually got lost walking to my seat. This was going on throughout the whole sanctuary—women rejoicing, crying, and giving everything to God so He could heal and renew us in each way we needed. So much was shared that weekend. We were able to pray with each other and truly bond. The saying "sisters in Christ" was always appealing to me. I liked the sound of it; it was fun. But, wow, this brought it all to life. We are sisters, praying, hugging, hurting for each other. The bond remained when we got back to church. It was a time we will never forget. It is so hard to get to know each other in the halls of church or a Bible study, but this time of fellowship—or I'll call it sistership—was unique and fun. We are so blessed to live in a country where we can meet as a group of women who love and want to serve God. I pray this freedom will never be taken from us.

Part VII

Overflow with Love

Aletha Hinthorn

How dearly God loves us because he has given us the Holy Spirit to fill our hearts with his love (Romans 5:5).

"God's love has been poured out into our hearts through the Holy Spirit, who has been given to us" (Romans 5:5 NIV). God desires to fill us with His unconditional, never failing love. He longs for us to receive and live in His love. When we begin to understand the extent of God's love, we no longer need a list of do's and don'ts. Out of our overflowing affection for Him, we hunger to show Him our love in all we do.

"May you experience the love of Christ, though it is too great to understand fully. Then you will be made complete with all the fullness of life and power that comes from God" (Ephesians 3:19).

Chapter 13

Infused with His Love

Kim McLean[1]

For God, who said, "Let light shine out of darkness," made his light shine in our hearts to give us the light of the knowledge of the glory of God in the face of Christ (II Corinthians 4:6).

Looking into the face of Jesus sounds wonderfully awesome, unless you take a look with a heart that isn't ready. Then you'll get a hard look at yourself instead, and it might just be a little like Moses not knowing to take off his shoes standing on the holy ground before God's burning presence. Scarier still is the way one eye-to-eye, heart-to-heart moment with Jesus will invite Him right into the midst of your darkness, and suddenly, "He who knew no sin became sin" turns into something about you and your sin. Sometimes you meet Jesus in the most unlikely places.

God is very insistent about the true condition of our hearts. Psalm 37, verse 4 says to delight yourself in the Lord. Good things happen when you delight yourself in the Lord. Then God will give you the desires of your heart. I think first you have to ask what the desires of your heart are; controlling those desires is another story. It's easy to say one thing, the right thing, and secretly harbor another.

The world loves those words—delight and desire. But the Bible uses those words unabashedly to describe what our relationship with the Lord is to be like. For me, all sorts of things can get tangled up in these two words. First of all, I have not always desired what was good for me. And telling me to delight in something holy was like telling me to delight in Brussels sprouts. You either like a thing or you don't, but how do you just decide to delight in something? How do you delight in Someone you don't know? And for many, delighting in God makes little sense when He seems to allow so much trouble. And if delighting in God means loving all people, even the ones who have hurt you the worst, then the whole deal gets even less delightful.

I have learned the hard way that I do not want God to give me the desires of my heart until they are lined up with His desires. And that happens in a moment of grace and over a lifetime.

I used to wonder how anyone ever ended up in church if they were not first broken. I saw it as sort of a soul hospital. And so it is. But then I met a few church people here and there who were the real deal, who had never strayed from the straight and narrow, who walked gracefully through the worst trials of life without complaining, whose countenance and godly character must have had the hosts of heaven approving with humble applause. Have you seen those saints whose heart's desire is so in tune with the Lord's that the mere mention of Jesus brings tears to their eyes? Those are the saints who get me "longing to long for more." The bright reflection they cast revealed my own dark cravings. In them, I saw the face of Jesus.

I used to ask God every day why I wanted to run toward the darkness. It was a restlessness that would tug at me. If I found any relief from the drive to darkness, it was short-lived. You can't conjure up firm resolve and walk in holy love. God has to change your nature. After three divorces, nearly dying of an eating disorder, alcohol abuse, and battles with depression, I was broken. That's the story that my drive to darkness created. And I did it all by myself. But hitting bottom wasn't what drove me to church. Maybe it is for some people. But sin and despair have a way of making us want to hide from God. There is no fear of hell when you think you deserve it. That's what shame does.

God has a real affinity for broken hearts, even when we have created our own messy pain. He waits to pick up the pieces, to help us out of the pit, and He longs to show us compassion. But it was not brokenness that made me love God. It was not failure or desperation. It was not the promise of a better life or even the promise of heaven. I love God because I can't help it. I love God because somehow, in the midst of my darkest night and my vilest desire, He got through to me with a whisper, with a heart-cry of His own—that He wanted me to be His, completely His. And in a moment, and then another moment, and another, of divine revelation, I knew what the church people knew, the real ones, and it is this: they know that they are precious in God's sight, treasured, loved beyond belief. And I fell in love with the Lord.

There is not a darkness dark enough that God cannot infuse with His light. This is how creation was born, and this is how He makes a new creation out of me. He doesn't just point a light into the darkness; He creates light from out of the darkness. He changes it, transforms it, permeates it with light. Resentment becomes forgiveness. Hatred becomes love. Fear becomes faith.

Vengeance becomes compassion. Pride becomes humility. Shame becomes blamelessness; and it's all because holiness becomes love.

I was having coffee with my friend Sam Green at Trevecca Nazarene University one day, and we were talking about holiness. He said, "Holiness is not something God wants from you; it's something He wants for you." I cried like the church people. You see, I couldn't make myself clean and holy; it's something God did. The best I had was pretty tragic, and at the bidding of His heart, I offered my worst to Him. This is when you learn what dying to live is all about. All of me for all of God means everything changes—all of you for all of God—your desires, your needs, your perspectives, your attitudes, your life.

Dreams come alive when you're not spending all your time trying to get it right or trying to get over things. There can be joy in the journey when we live it as God created it to be.

There is a choice we make that ushers in the light and pokes a hole in the black tapestry we have tried to hide behind. It is the choice to love the Lord whole-heartedly, and so the light invades the darkness in our lives, pervades the secret places. This is how we begin to be infused with His love. It begins with repentance, honesty, coming clean—once and for all, again and again.

"Create in me a clean heart, Oh God, and renew a right spirit within me. Cast me not away from your presence, and take not your Holy Spirit from me" (Psalm 51:10-11 ESV). David knew about the brokenness that longs for a holy heart when he prayed those words. Because He was in love with the Lord, he knew that nothing would be as devastating as losing that relationship or losing sight of God's precious presence.

In Psalm 51, he prayed a prayer of repentance after he'd done terrible things. His prayer will grip you to the core if you've ever failed love. "Have mercy on me, O God, according to your steadfast love, according to your abundant mercy blot out my transgressions. Wash me thoroughly from my iniquity, and cleanse me from my sin" (Psalm 51:1-2 ESV). He prayed, not just with remorse, but with a repentant heart. How would he ever live with himself after what he had done? He acknowledged his sin and God's authority. "Behold, you delight in truth in the inward being, and you teach me wisdom in the secret heart" (Psalm 51:6 ESV). David reached a broken place. Broken, not just because of His sin and failure; broken, not because he was in big trouble; but broken because He broke the heart of God, the one his soul loved. He'd broken love's command.

But God listened. And God heard. And God forgave —just like He pardoned Paul for persecuting the church people; just like He did Peter for denying Him; just like He does you and me when we seek His face. He will not despise a broken and contrite heart,[2] and He will not break a bruised reed.[3] He longs to show us compassion. God has this gentle, fierce way of killing us with kindness, of reassuring us of His unfailing love while demanding that we walk in righteousness, which only He can empower us to do. Ironic, isn't it? We surrender; He sets us free.

We are not free to be good, or clean, or holy, or barely even alive, without God's grace. God wants hearts that are, as Beth Coppedge says, "squeaky clean," that reflect Him as hearts are meant to do. It is not God's will that we live in hopelessness or bitterness, resentment or fear. We need His cleansing power to heal our sins and shortcomings but also to cleanse our hearts with forgiveness for the ones who have hurt us or for the memories that keep us in bondage

God wants us to be clean, to have clean hearts, and to live clean, holy lives in all our affairs. It shows. God's love shows in your life by the way you talk, the things you spend your time doing, the way you take care of your health, the way you pay your bills on time. All of you belongs to God, seven days a week, twenty-four hours a day. Paul said it best when preaching in Athens: "In Him we live and move and have our being."[4]

It feels good to seek the warmth of His love instead of always hanging on to the "I'll be happy whens" or a million regrets from the past. God wants you to look in the mirror and see a treasure instead of a disaster.

Sometimes I think about the story where the woman was caught in adultery and Jesus said, "Let those without sin cast the first stone."[5] I wonder if He meant "those without big sins like the woman's" or did He mean even the little secret sins. Little sins are like the little foxes that come in to destroy the vine and ruin the sweet fruit of love, joy, peace, patience, kindness, faithfulness, self-control, goodness.[6] It's the little things, little attitudes, little perspectives, little fears, little thoughts that begin to quench the Spirit and the good life God has for us.

We are called out to be holy, that is to say wholly-His, completely overtaken by the love of God, so full that the living water within us "sloshes over" and blesses God's beautiful world. Beth Coppedge likes to say, "God doesn't need clever vessels. He needs clean ones." We are salt. We are light. God wants to work in us and through us in this world to fill it with His love. My friend Brother Spruill says, "If God's only goal for us were Heaven, He'd save us and then take us on home right then and there." It's when we get in line with God's loving will that eternal life begins here and now, and we become participants in His plan to heal the nations, one squeaky clean heart at a time.

Paul says to declare that we have a treasure, the treasure of God, in earthen vessels. "But we have this treasure in jars of clay to show that this all surpassing power belongs to God and not to us" (II Corinthians 4:7 NIV). We are like the clay jars they used in the first century. The clay jars he referred to were fragile, and when archeologists find them, they are broken in pieces. Those vessels of clay carried the day-to-day things, the water, the food, things that helped keep them alive. God does not despise what is broken. He uses it. And we are called to carry the living water of love day by day, in the normal circumstances, in the normal places, moment by moment where life happens.

I guess even church people without a dark past get broken because it's a matter of the heart, and there is not one of us that can shine with the brightness of His glory without His grace. But there is also a brokenness that comes when God's overflowing love crashes in on our complacency and says, "I've called you to love the world like I love it." God breaks our complacent hearts. Our heart breaks for the lost and for the hurting and for the nations who don't yet know about the God of peace. We don't just come to church and hide within the safety of these walls while the world perishes. We are called to make a difference in this world with God's love. We are called to set the world on fire with revival!

God says it over and over, from beginning to end of the Bible: Love the Lord with all your heart. Delight in Him. Set your heart and mind on Him. Love Him. Verse after verse He tells how to let that love happen. It's like a seed planted in the sacred ground that must first die before it grows new life. You eek out a prayer, or maybe you shout it to heaven, but it's a heart cry, "Jesus come to me." You ask Him to give you an undivided heart, the gift of His love. Then the fleshly desires die, and the Spirit gives life and empowers you to live it. Light infuses the darkness and overtakes the chaos to create something amazing and real.

Frederick Buechner wrote, "In the end, the command to love God is not so much a command as it is a promise." I think of the verse in Song of Solomon that says, "Many waters cannot quench love, neither can the floods drown it" (Song of Solomon 8:7 ESV). Not long ago, we sang at a small church in Ashland City, Tennessee, and a lady named Ellie walked up to me, pressed a small piece of paper in my hand, and whispered: "Nothing can quench your love for the Lord." I cried like the church people again. I so wanted that to be true, that my Beloved has such a seal on my heart that nothing can ever sway me from His Presence. The paper Ellie handed to me was the verse from the Song of Songs. She passed away suddenly only a few days later, and I realized that I had had one of those "glory of God in the face of Jesus" moments.

Loving God sets things right. Giving Him your whole heart ultimately captivates your attention and your desires. We love God with the love He puts within us. Loving God is an act of grace. We say "yes" to God, and He reaches right into the darkest of nights and transforms it. He rewrites our story and tells the truth about us from a new, holy, squeaky clean perspective. He empowers us to love each other that way, too. A story that was ugly and sad becomes, instead, a love-story, His story.

My story is not mine anymore. It's His. You have to decide to let God do the telling.

Sometimes it's hard for you to see how precious you
are
But there in the dark He's reaching to take you by the
hand
You're never alone, your heart is His home, your value
is in Him
And He loves you, He loves You—His golden light is
pouring in

YOU HAVE A TREASURE
IN A VESSEL OF CLAY
YOU WERE FORMED TO HOLD
THE POWER OF HIS GLORY
YOU'RE A STORY OF HIS GRACE

Sometimes it's hard for you to see the gift of His
presence
Troubles surround you—seems like you're pressed on
every side
He's made you whole—you can let go and trust in His
promise
It's a mystery, it's the beauty, the miracle of holy life

YOU HAVE A TREASURE
IN A VESSEL OF CLAY
YOU WERE FORMED TO HOLD
THE POWER OF HIS GLORY
YOU'RE A STORY OF HIS GRACE

Let's give thanks.
Thank you, Lord
I love you!

I HAVE A TREASURE

IN A VESSEL OF CLAY
I WAS FORMED TO HOLD
THE POWER OF HIS GLORY
I'M A STORY OF HIS GRACE

God saved you by his grace when you believed. And you can't take credit for this; it is a gift from God. Salvation is not a reward for the good things we have done, so none of us can boast about it. For we are God's masterpiece. He has created us anew in Christ Jesus, so we can do the good things he planned for us long ago (Ephesians 2:8-10).

Chapter 14

Revive Our Nation

Nancy Jesudass[1]

If my people, who are called by My Name, will humble themselves and pray and seek my face and turn from their wicked ways, then I will hear from heaven, and I will forgive their sin and will heal their land (II Chronicles 7:14 NIV).

I owe my life to Americans. I would like to tell you why. One day, over a hundred years ago, a young man was wandering in the streets of Hanoi, North Vietnam, looking for a way to commit suicide. At that very moment, an American missionary "happened" to appear before him and offered him a gospel tract. He had no interest in the tract but politely took it and put it in his pocket without any intention of reading it.

This young man wanted to end his life. He didn't love the wife his parents had forced him to marry. He was addicted to opium. Each day, after finishing his work at the office, he would go straight to an opium den and spend many hours there. Eventually, he would head home around midnight. That was his daily routine for about two years. One evening in the opium den, the gospel tract that had been given to him by the missionary fell out from his pocket. He picked it up and casually read it just to pass the time. He became interested in the message contained within the tract. He looked for a local church to inquire more about this Jesus he had just read about. With the help of the pastor, this young man became a follower of Jesus. He got rid of the opium and began a new life, seeking to love his wife as Christ loves the Church. After that he led his wife as well as all of his children to Jesus. That young man was my father. I was born years later as one of his eight children. My father was a man of prayer and served the Lord wholeheartedly until the day he died.

As the gospel of Jesus was brought to Vietnam, thousands just like my father were saved. Because of the love and sacrifices of Christians in America and the fervent prayers and devotion to Jesus of many of your forefathers, there have been numerous people like me who have now given their lives to full-time service for the Kingdom of God. And that is why I mentioned to you earlier that I owe you Americans and your ancestors my very life.

I came to America in 1970 with much admiration for this great nation, and I rejoiced as I witnessed the glory of God upon America. I enjoyed the blessings as well. However, as the days went by, especially in the late 80's, I began to notice the moral decay and the spiritual downfall slowly gripping this lovely land—the land that attracted the whole world! I found myself becoming deeply grieved at what I was witnessing. I shed many tears as I painfully saw more and more decline year after year.

One day in early 1990, while I was walking with Jesus in a solitary lane as was my usual routine, suddenly I found myself standing still. I heard a voice, not audible, but loud and clear from within me. I felt the voice say to me, "Nancy, are you willing to give up your part time job and the activities in the church and go into full time intercession? I'm calling you to be an intercessor, especially focused on revival of America. Are you willing?"

I was in awe of His presence and was speechless. I knew He was calling me to a service that I felt so utterly unworthy of! At that moment, I couldn't comprehend it all, but I knew it was Jesus walking beside me and talking to me. His voice was so clear and so dear. By then my face was covered with tears! It was almost dark as I walked back home. No one was home when I arrived so I continued to be alone in His presence. I sat down in my living room and began to respond to Him. I said, "Yes, Lord, may it be to me as You have said." I knew this was Mary's response when she was visited by the angel Gabriel.

Since receiving that call more than twenty years ago now, I have prayed earnestly for revival upon our nation. Sometimes I pray for hours and hours at a time. To this very day, I have continued to pray for revival which would lead to the Great Commission, for our God is the God of the nations.

When I found myself groaning in prayer, I came to understand that it was Jesus who was travailing through me. The Lord did multiply intercessors. Wherever I went, I would find other like-minded women, and we would join together in crying out for an outpouring of the Living Water upon this weary and thirsty land.

Now, I want to share with you something that I had never shared publicly before this year. It is something I had only shared with a few close friends in my inner circle. In the beginning of 2012, I felt God impressed upon my heart that I was to share this whenever I was given an opportunity, so I obeyed. In January of 1998 God called me to a forty day fast, drinking only water and one glass of clear juice each day. I didn't discuss this with my flesh and blood but simply obeyed what I believed God was asking me to do. One doctor who happened to know about the fast, told me, "Nancy, if you lose twenty pounds you might die." And I did lose twenty pounds.

A year later, the Lord called me to fast again for forty days in the same manner but in two periods of twenty days at a time. Again, I obeyed His voice. The next year, He said to me again that I was to fast for another forty days in the same manner but this time in four separate segments of ten days at a time. Again, I did what I believed He was asking me to do. During each fast, amazingly, I never experienced any sign of sickness such as a stomachache, headache or dizziness. What I did experience with God through those days was His heart crying through me for this nation to repent, beginning with the house of God. But the more I cried through those years, the more I saw this nation continuing to get worse and worse with little repentance.

In 2001, after 9/11, I said to God, "O Lord, this time, we'll surely humble ourselves before you and repent." And yes, there was some repentance here and there, but it seemed to only last for a short while. It seemed like it was very similar to what the prophet Hosea was saying to the Israelites: "Your love is like the morning mist, like the early dew that disappears" (Hosea 6:4 NIV).

I tried to figure out why God might be delaying in answering our prayers and, moreover, there seemed to be more calamity and even judgment on the nations. I found many of the prophets in the Old Testament asked God the same thing at times, and His response was, "Thus will

I spend My wrath upon them. Then you will know that I am the LORD...." (Ezekiel 6:12-13 NASB).

I realized that was God's stubborn love! He does not leave us alone but continues to pursue us until we respond to Him. In the book of Judges and all throughout the Old Testament, we read that when God's people did evil in the eyes of the Lord, God gave them into the hands of the enemy. "But when they cried out to the LORD, He raised up for them a deliverer...." (Judges 3:9 NIV).

He is ready to deliver us if we cry out to Him in brokenness and repentance. Today, God is still calling out to us, "If my people, who are called by my name, will humble themselves and pray and seek my face and turn from their wicked ways, then will I hear from heaven, and will forgive their sin and will heal their land" (II Chronicles 7:14 NIV).

We repeat this so often in our prayers and even hear it over and over again from the pulpit, but so far no serious action has truly taken place. We do not seem to be desperate enough for God.

Today in our nation we have witnessed or experienced so much distress in so many families. Children become victims as a result of broken homes; we see more defeat than victory in our churches, in our community, on school campuses, and in the market place. We are drowning as a nation so rapidly, especially in the last decade. We are in desperate need of God's intervention. The glory of God is no longer upon us! The nations around us seem to ask, "Where is your God?" In fact, inside my spirit I feel I can hear the lost around me crying out to us as the church like the people cried out to Jonah, "How can you sleep? Get up and call on your god! Maybe he will take notice of us that we will not perish" (Jonah 1:6 NIV).

Let us look deeply into our nation and incline our ear to hear the cries of the children, teenagers, and adults who are starving for the Bread of Life. Many attempt to satisfy their hunger by the junk food offered so readily through television, computers, and other forms of media. Let us take time today to pause and listen to cries of the poor, those who are hungry and starving. Six million children die in the world every day because of starvation.

Let us hear the cries of men and woman around us who are suffering under bondages of different kinds. All of us can name the addictions that are entrapping so many—drugs, alcohol, pornography, etc.

Each of us needs to personally ask ourselves a few questions: Right now, am I sleeping? Am I still looking for comfort, needing to wake up? Am I aware of the cries of prisoners around me? Am I ignoring them?

Perhaps some of you are suffering personally under bondage, and you need to be set free as well.

May God forgive us as leaders, as shepherds of the flock. We seem to prefer lecturing over suffering and spend such little time crying out to God on behalf of ourselves, our families, our churches, and our nation. May God forgive us all.

Now, may I ask you to close your eyes for a minute and let us take a brief journey to the garden of Gethsemane? Let's look at your Savior who prostrated himself before God crying out for you and me. The author of Hebrews says that Jesus offered up prayer and petition on our behalf with loud cries and tears to God[2] and His sweat which became like blood fell to the ground. And hear what Jesus said to His disciples: "Are you still sleeping? Get up and pray."[3]

At the crucifixion, a group of women followed Jesus. They cried and mourned for Him, but Jesus said to them,

"Daughters of Jerusalem, do not weep for me; weep for yourselves and for your children" (Luke 23:28 NIV).

The Bible says that when the people in Nineveh cried to the Lord, the Lord saved this wicked nation because of their humbleness and repentant hearts.[4]

The enemy has entered into our homes, into our churches, into our educational systems, into our government as well as into our economy. Our nation is like an open wound without protection because God has seemed to remove the hedge of protection around us.

We are in deep trouble not any less than Nineveh. Let us humble ourselves and repent—repent for ourselves, repent for our children, repent for our family, repent for the church, repent for our nation, repent for the world!

Now my eyes will be open and my ears attentive to the prayers offered in this place. I have chosen and consecrated this temple so that my Name may be there forever. My eyes and my heart will always be there (II Chronicles 7:15-16 NIV).

Prayer by Nancy at Come to the Fire in October 2014

Oh, Father, our nation right now is like a flickering candle. How we need Your intervention so desperately! Father in heaven, as Daniel was interceding for the nation of Israel in a most critical time, I want to join his prayer for our nation "for such a time as this!

"Oh, Lord, You are a great and awesome God! You always fulfill your covenant and keep your promises of unfailing love to those who love you and obey your commands. But we have sinned and done wrong. We have rebelled against you and scorned your commands and regulations. We have refused to listen to your servants the prophets" (Daniel 9:4-6).

Oh, Father, I confess to You that as a nation we have committed idolatry. We have worshipped images of our own pleasures instead of worshipping You, our Maker, our Redeemer. We have forsaken the Fountain of Life. As a nation, we have committed adultery through many forms of sexual sins. We have murdered unborn babies. We have allowed our homes to be broken. We have led our children astray.

Oh, Lord, You are righteous, but our faces are covered with shame because we have turned our back to You. We have caused the nations around us to stumble and confused them of what we claim to be as a nation under God, a nation that honors your name! We have been an object of mockery! Therefore, the nations constantly ask us, "Where is your God?" Yes, Father, we have defiled Your name, Your holy name! But, oh, Father, You are a forgiving God. You are gracious; You are compassionate, slow to anger and abounding in love. Even though we run away from You, You keep pursuing us because of Your unfailing love!

Yes, Father, we have truly defiled Your name! But we thank You for Your promise to us that "if my people, who are called by My name, will humble themselves and pray and seek My face and turn from their wicked way, then I will hear from heaven. I will forgive their sins and will heal their land" (II Chronicles 7:14 NIV).

So here we are! Abba, Abba Father! We humble ourselves before You as the church, the bride of Christ. We repent of our sins that we have not been salt and light to preserve our land as we are called to be. As Your church, we repent of our prayerlessness, of our complacency. We repent of our reluctance in reaching out to the lost. We ask that You would revive our nation. We pray for our government leaders that they will seek Your face and turn to You for wisdom and guidance to lead the nation in the way of the Lord.

We ask that You would renew our church, the body of Jesus Christ on earth. May You cause the book of Acts to become alive in our midst again. May we be like the believers in the early church to whom You outpoured Your Spirit. You said through the prophet Isaiah, "I'll pour water on the thirsty land, streams on the dry ground. I'll pour out My Spirit on your offspring and My blessing on your descendants."[5] Oh, God, how we long to experience the outpouring of Your Spirit upon us, the body of Christ, and upon our thirsty land. Oh, Father, may our neighbors see the Fire of Your Spirit through us causing them to run and ask: "What must I do to be saved?"

Father in heaven, we will not forget to bring to You other nations that are on Your heart right now. We pray for Israel. We pray for Syria, for the Ukraine, for North Korea, for Iraq, and for all other nations as well! Oh, Father, may all people soon find Jesus as Prince of Peace. May Your salvation be made known among them, Father!

We especially pray for Your church in Iraq. We pray for our brothers and sisters to stand firm in the name of Jesus. May they be found loyal to Jesus. May You give them strength and courage to endure the sufferings. Oh, Abba, may Your grace be sufficient for them. I pray that many unbelievers will find salvation through the witness of those suffering for Your name. May Your name be made known and be honored through their persecution.

Oh, may God rend the heavens and come down that the nations will tremble before You. Come down, O mighty God, come down and make Your name known to the enemies. Abba Father, right now our nation seems to walk through the valley of the shadow of darkest moments, but we are not afraid for You are with us. You said, "I'm with you always till the end of the age."[6] Father, please set a table before us now in the presence of our enemies. For Your name's sake, O Lord, revive us as a nation; renew us as a church, Your bride. Purify Your bride. We make this plea not because we deserve Your help, but because of your mercies and love. Oh, Lord, hear and forgive! Listen and act! For Your name's sake, do not delay, oh my God. We are Your people, the people that love Your name. We pray in the name of Jesus, the Lamb of God, who has taken our sins away. Amen.

Glimpses of Grace

CTTF Attendees

Overflowing with Forgiveness

I am changed through the inspiration and encouragement of hearing the message of living a life totally surrendered to Jesus Christ. God brought to my attention someone I have been struggling with emotionally. When I came forward for prayer, the lady who prayed for me had the exact words I needed to hear at that moment to forgive this person. God is alive and working through this ministry! Praise His Holy Name!

Overflowing with Freedom

It was my first Come to the Fire. I really didn't know what to expect, but it was everything I needed, down to the people staying in my room. My heart was transformed. I have the relationship with the Lord I have always wanted. Praise Jesus! I am so blessed. I was never able to say that! I am free at last from the past! Praise God!

Overflowing with Christ

This was my first year attending Come to the Fire, and Lord willing, it will not be my last. The Lord used each song and speaker to prepare my heart for what He would whisper. Because of this, it was obvious that every aspect of the event had been continually prayed over—even I was prayed over. Come to the Fire equipped me to walk back into my home confidently, knowing what God had spoken intimately to me, and that His words for me would not return void.

Overflowing with His Presence

I am humbled, encouraged, amazed, and very, very grateful for His powerful presence at the conference. What an experience! I felt like we were standing by the burning bush with our shoes off, and He was very near by! Women left challenged to spread the Fire He had ignited and rekindled in our hearts.

Overflowing with His Spirit

I am so thankful to be a part of a women's conference that focuses corporately on prayer and worship as well as hearing the preaching and testimonies from women who are humbly walking with Him. Our time at Come to the Fire was spent seeking Jesus and the infilling of His Holy Spirit. Jesus died for each of us making us all equal, and we enjoy glorious fellowship with one another. It is such a special experience to know that the sanctuary where we worship is filled with women from so many states as well as other countries and multiple denominations. We only know one another because of our common love and devotion to Christ. I am reminded that on the day of Pentecost the Holy Spirit came as the believers were all in one place praying. They were in one accord—much like our experience at Come to the Fire. The words that have kept coming to my mind during the conference and during the days since are glorious and peaceful.

Overflowing with Holy Desires

The session on intercession was amazing. God spoke to my heart very clearly that I have been sinning in this area. I have desired and strived to be like Jesus, but never have made the connection that Jesus intercedes with the Father, so I should also. I have determined to make this a priority. I have started to awaken a half hour earlier to pray for the people around me and for my country.

Overflowing with Healing

I have had incredible encounters with Christ through Come to the Fire. The conference in 2012 was the beginning of healing from seven years of depression. God's still small voice asked me to clean up some unhealthy relationships, and by being obedient to Him, I have been able to overcome and be completely healed from depression. Jesus is my healer and my strength. This Come to the Fire conference has helped me to be able to pray, "Jesus, fill me so much with Yourself that there is nothing left of me; for if there is anything left of me, I won't be holy." I want to be holy because He is holy.

Overflowing with a God-given Identity

During the healing service, we were invited to pray and ask the Spirit to speak to us. I was pouring out my heart to the Lord with such questions as, "Why don't I feel enough, Lord? I can't be enough at home, at church, with my friends, at work. I just feel like I'm not enough! Are You enough, Lord? I know you are, but can I ask, 'Are you really enough?'" Melinda then invited us to sing a song about our identity as a daughter of the Father, and she said, "Ladies, this morning, you are enough in Christ, and He is enough for you." God answered my cries almost immediately, and His voice literally took my breath away. I praise Him that He is enough and makes me complete in Christ Jesus. He is truly my ever present Help, Word, Comfort, and Song! Thank you, Lord! And thank you, Melinda, for flowing in radical obedience to the Holy Spirit.

Part VIII

Celebrate Your Freedom

Aletha Hinthorn

...you will know the truth, and the truth will set you free....So if the Son sets you free, you will be free indeed (John 8:32, 36 NIV).

Imagine living free from bondages! If we abandon ourselves to obey His great and precious promises, we will discover a life of peace and liberty. Rather than striving to follow a list of rules, we'll know the freedom of living a joyful Spirit-led life.

For when we died with Christ we were set free from the power of sin (Romans 6:7).

Chapter 15

Celebrating My Freedom
Darcy Dill[1]

The LORD doesn't see things the way you see them. People judge by outward appearance, but the LORD looks at the heart (I Samuel 16:7).

I was the youngest of five girls born in Brazil, South America, where my parents were serving as missionaries. It was hard to be so much younger than my sisters because they thought I wasn't old enough to go places with them and would be in the way, keeping them from having fun. I felt that my opinion didn't count when making family decisions and that no one really cared what I thought or how I felt because I had the least amount of education and experience. When I did something wrong and got in trouble, I felt guilt and shame; thus, at an early age, I sensed that I needed to earn my acceptance and prove my value.

Unfortunately, that overflowed into the rest of my life. Being a tall, fair-skinned American with long, blonde hair in a country filled with mostly shorter people with dark skin and hair, I stood out and got a lot of attention. I learned early that looks are important for acceptance. People judge you by your looks.

As I got older, I wanted to wear make-up so I could look pretty. I always thought I looked like an ugly duckling because with blonde hair I didn't have distinguished features, and I felt that make-up would make my features stand out. It seemed to work because I got a lot of attention; people were always complimenting me on my looks so I figured I needed to always wear cosmetics to be acceptable. When someone said, "You'll lose all your friends if you cut your hair," and a boyfriend said, "I'm not sure I could marry you because I don't know what you look like without your make-up," that sealed it for me! I knew I could never go anywhere without having my make-up and hair looking perfect!

This led to a life of always trying to look perfect and working hard to please everyone in order to earn their acceptance. It was devastating to think that someone might not like me or would say something negative about me!

In 1986 my husband and I began our first pastorate. Now I had a whole congregation to try to please. I couldn't feel comfortable anywhere because we were now living in the "fishbowl." It felt like all eyes were on us, and it seemed there were a lot of unspoken expectations! Before our first Sunday there, the Christian Education Director asked if I would be willing to substitute teach a children's Sunday School class. I had never taught anything in my life before! I had zero experience being a leader! As a kid that was voted most shy in high school, his request took me way out of my comfort zone! After several years I became depressed but didn't understand what was going on with me. I only knew I was miserable.

I took secular jobs hoping to impact people's lives for Christ. Most of the jobs were in some kind of customer service which gave me a whole new batch of people I had to please—not to mention trying to raise two boys who were active in many sports. I also took on a new venture of real estate investing and had several tenants to please. In all of this striving to people-please, I went through seasons of severe depression. At the time I didn't understand why I was depressed. I just knew I wanted the world to stop and let me off—to move to a deserted island and be a hermit where no one would have expectations of me and I wouldn't have the overwhelming feeling of obligation to everyone.

I considered my people pleasing to be good, a servant thing. One day I heard someone say they had been a people pleaser, too, and how self-centered that was. What a shock to me! As I pondered that thought, it became apparent that my motivation for trying to please others was not servanthood but that others would like me and I would be accepted! I was crushed and mortified at this revelation and felt so ashamed! My whole reason for existence was self motivated! My focus was on me all the time! I always worried about what others thought and constantly tried to protect myself from being hurt, all while trying so hard to stay in my own comfort zone.

As a pastor's wife I always had my foot on the brakes not wanting to take on any leadership role for fear someone might criticize me. I didn't like meeting new people because I couldn't remember their names. It seemed overwhelming to have to get to know so many people and try to keep up with all their lives, their illnesses, the deaths of loved ones, and much more. Invitations to parties made me miserable. I felt I wasn't funny or witty enough, that I wasn't well versed in world events, and I was definitely out of it when it came to sports. It seemed there was an unwritten code or a role I had to play in being a pastor's wife. I felt I had to pretend to be something I wasn't but what everyone else wanted me to be.

After trying to please people in three pastorates and working at jobs where there was a constant flow of customers to please, not to mention my family, life was too hard. I couldn't handle it anymore. Yes, I'll have to admit the thought of suicide even entered my head. Actually, I ran off one night to a secluded place to get away and think of what my options were to get out of my misery. Thankfully, the Lord instilled enough of His thoughts in me to keep me from doing any of the extreme things that entered my mind.

I had grown up playing the guitar and always wondered if God was going to use it for some greater purpose. When my church needed someone to play the bass guitar, my knowledge made me the go-to person even though I had never played the bass and didn't have a clue where any of the notes were. Someone drew a fret map of the notes, and after I practiced a little, in about three weeks I was up front playing with our worship band. I always thought I was just a fill-in until they could find someone who could really play.

One day while playing at my church, I had an episode that felt like a panic attack in the middle of worship. I became fearful it might happen again, and I might pass out and bring attention to myself. That would be embarrassing! So, I took several months off from playing bass.

During that time Melinda Priest asked me to play for Come to the Fire in 2008. I wasn't sure I could do it. While trying to decide if I should go or not, I came across the verse that says, "So do not fear, for I am with you; do not be dismayed, for I am your God. I will strengthen you and help you; I will uphold you with my righteous right hand" (Isaiah 41:10 NIV).

I decided I'd go and trust the Lord. That year one message told about God giving Jacob a new name. Jacob means Deceiver. The new name God gave him was Israel, which means you have struggled with God and men and have overcome. God showed me that my old name was Personal Preserver. I was always protecting myself from rejection or criticism. The new name God gave me was Recklessly Abandoned to God! And I do believe that's how God wants me to live! With complete faith, hope, and trust in Him—all my eggs in one basket! No reservations! No cushion and no Plan B!

I struggled through all the sessions. I'd feel the Lord speaking to me during the messages but would fight back the tears. After all, I'd have to go up and play in a short while and didn't want to have a messy face with half my make-up cried off. So I never really gave in and let the Lord do His work in me at that time—still being worried about what other people would think.

In April 2011, Melinda asked me to play for a Women Clergy Conference. I was again struggling with a bout of depression and anxiety. The decision whether to go or not was very difficult. My husband, Mark, who was away at a conference, sent me a text message saying that he had been praying for me and felt that God was saying to him that I should go, that God wanted to heal me. That scared me! What did that mean? What would God want from me if he healed me? After all, God doesn't heal a person just for their comfort; He always expects something in return, doesn't He, I mused?

Maybe I don't want to be healed. Perhaps what God would expect of me would be worse than what I'm going through now. I've been here so long it almost feels comfortable; this struggling person that's always seeking, always striving, has been my identity. My bookshelves are full of self-help books from a lifetime of searching for answers to why I struggle so much. Why am I so unhappy? What is wrong with me? How do I find peace? There's got to be more. Isn't there a magic formula or a pill that would fix me and I'd be okay? Then I'd be happy and confident and acceptable to everyone?

Then I looked down at my open Bible, and right in the middle of the page where I had previously underlined was the verse, "'For I know the plans I have for you,' declares the LORD, 'plans to prosper you and not to harm you, plans to give you hope and a future'" (Jeremiah 29:11 NIV). That was my answer; I should go and trust the Lord.

I did go, and God continued working in me through my thoughts, conversations by phone with my husband, and prayers with Melinda and others at the conference. One prayer that was prayed over me was, "Lord, cover Darcy with the blood of Jesus and fill her with your Spirit."

Then I prayed, "Lord, please forgive me of any unconfessed sin in my life and cleanse me from all unrighteousness. Please help me with my over-thinking mind as I over-analyze everything. I'm double-minded and so insecure. Lord, please speak my love language of affirmation. I need your reassurance and your approval. Please give me boldness, courage, and God-confidence. And, Lord, I don't know what you want to do in my life, but as scary as it seems to me, I care more about what You think of me than what others think. I want to live to please you more than pleasing others. Help me to do that. So I submit myself to you and your will! Help me to fall in love with you! I want to be able to read and understand your Word and have a passion for it! And thank You in advance for what you are going to do. Amen."

That was tough! There was no lightning bolt, no strange occurrences, just peace. Suddenly we realized we were running late for the practice for the next service so we rushed to get ready. I threw on some clothes and dabbed on make-up, ran out the door and barely caught the elevator the other ladies were holding for me. I said, "Whew! I rushed so fast, am I even dressed?"

Then I looked down and saw I had put on two different colored shoes. They were black and light brown! Thoughts ran through my mind of how long it would take to ride the elevator back up six floors, change them and wait for the elevator again to ride back down, and then be late to the practice—all for the sake of vanity. So I said, "You know what? I'm goin' for it!"

Immediately, all the ladies on the elevator started cheering and clapping for me. They said things like, "Yay, Darcy! Freedom!" It felt like a big weight was lifted off my shoulders! Then as I walked around and up and down from the platform, which was eye level with those in the seats, I felt light as a feather. My heart just soared! It was Jesus and me, and I was doing what I thought would please Him and didn't care what other people thought. The service was wonderful! I played my heart out and just privately worshiped the Lord as I sang and played. The Lord's presence was so sweet!

At the end of the service while there were several praying at the altar, I no longer could follow the keyboardist so I set my bass down and just sat in my seat on the platform to pray. One of the ladies working with our team came onto the platform and quietly anointed each of us with oil. But she anointed our feet! When she came to me, she shrugged her shoulders and said, "I'm just doing this because I felt the Lord wanted me to do it."

Then I looked down at my mismatching shoes! She had no idea why she was supposed to do this, but it was clear to me! I felt such affirmation from the Lord! What a quick answer to prayer! He accepted my sacrifice of the two different colored shoes! The Lord was so gracious! I felt so much love from the Lord—so blessed beyond words! I wept and wept for joy. When I arrived back home, I couldn't wait to share my story with everyone.

God continued to gently reveal truth to me about my pride regarding outward appearance, and I walked in obedience, each time sensing a new measure of healing and freedom to be myself. As I have continued my love relationship with Him, the Lord has given me such a strong desire and passion for Him! He has helped me to see that I had been listening to the voice of the enemy, and not God's. I had believed the lies of Satan about my lack of value. He had kept me living in bondage to fear my whole life! I'm sad about all the lost years of living in darkness with fear. And if it wasn't fear, it was guilt over not measuring up to something or shame for not being able to be a better Christian or not sharing my faith. One thing I've learned is that Satan deals in condemnation, which makes us feel shame and guilt and holds us back. God is loving. He brings conviction to our hearts that draws us upward and forward. He affectionately calls to us with open arms extended.

My passion is to help others be released from the bondage of Satan and have freedom in Jesus. I want to help them see the truth of Satan's lies and to be overcomers through the power of the Holy Spirit. I want to be a deliverer, and I pray for God to bring others into my life who will join me in this battle against Satan.

What's amazing is the joy God has given me! I don't have to walk in fear of what people will think of me anymore or try to earn God's love or anyone else's. There's nothing I could ever do, or not do, to make Him love me more or less. He showed me that He loves me just as I am! What freedom! And He has a destiny for me that no one else can fulfill. God has done a transformation in my life! He turned my life of fear and misery into joy unspeakable and full of glory! To God be the glory!

Trust in the LORD *with all your heart; do not depend on your own understanding. Seek his will in all you do, and he will show you which path to take (Proverbs 3:5).*

Chapter 16

The Ministry of the Shining Faces

Beth Coppedge[1]

"Now it was so, when Moses came down from Mount Sinai (and the two tablets of the Testimony were in Moses' hand when he came down from the mountain), that Moses did not know that the skin of his face shone while he talked with Him. So when Aaron and all the children of Israel saw Moses, behold, the skin of his face shone, and they were afraid to come near him. Then Moses called to them, and Aaron and all the rulers of the congregation returned to him; and Moses talked with them. Afterward all the children of Israel came near, and he gave them as commandments all that the Lord had spoken with him on Mount Sinai. And when Moses had finished speaking with them, he put a veil on his face. But whenever Moses went in before the Lord to speak with Him, he would take the veil off until he came out; and he would come out and speak to the children of Israel whatever he had been commanded. And whenever the children of Israel saw the

face of Moses, that the skin of Moses' face shone, then Moses would put the veil on his face again, until he went in to speak with Him" (Exodus 34:29-35 NKJV).

Today I have the sweetest thing to share with you. It is about the ministry of the shining faces. When Moses came down from the mountain, he did not know that the skin of his face was glowing.

Prayer

Oh, Jesus, we praise You today. We praise You for Yourself. Truly, Lord Jesus, it is only in You that we want to give glory. You alone are worthy of our worship. Thank You for what You can do in every one of our lives. Thank You for the glory of Rahab's life. As she turned her face toward You, she never could have dreamed of the overwhelming goodness of God for one little woman who said "yes" to You. The whole world is blessed as she was the ancestor of the Lord Jesus Himself. Jesus, there is no telling what You want to do with the women in this room. So we come today, just like Samuel, saying, "Speak, Lord, for Your servant is listening." As You call each of us by name, would you quicken our hearts and say to us what You have to say? May we go forth from Your fellowship to be a fellowship of shining faces with no veil that would come between. We go from here into a world that isn't quite like Come to the Fire. I pray we would be full, led, empowered, and anointed by the Spirit of God—that there would be transformation every place we go because we are carriers of Your beautiful, divine Holy presence. Make us carriers today of Your presence because we are squeaky clean. Set us free. Let not one go away today that has any residual left of the old life or the chains or the old bondage. Let us leave them at the altar before we go forth so we can join the fellowship of the shining faces to touch a globe for God. We pray it in the name of the Father, in the name of the Son, and in the name of Your beautiful Holy Spirit. Amen.

Message

I haven't been out a lot for the past eighteen months, but I was going to Indian Springs Camp with Al this summer. When we were packed up and all ready, I went to tell my daddy good-bye. I ran to Papa and said, "What will we do? I feel overwhelmed about going to Indian Springs."

He chuckled and said, "Well, Bethie, I think the first thing you can do is get your pronouns straight."

I said, "What do you mean?"

He reminded me of the story in Numbers 20 when the people rebelled against Aaron and Moses complaining about no water and asking, "Why did you bring us here to die?"

Moses and Aaron went to the entrance of the tabernacle, fell with their faces on the ground, and the glory of the Lord fell on them. The Lord told them to assemble the people and take the rod. He said, "As the people watch, speak to the rock over there, and it will pour out its water."[2]

Moses did as he was told. He took the rod and summoned the people. He shouted, "Must we bring you water from this rock?"[3] Then he struck the rock twice with the staff. He was frustrated and overwhelmed and mixed up his pronouns.

We are going home from CTTF to many different states—even different countries. God has met us here. It is as if we are coming down from the mountain with shining faces. Maybe we will be going to contentious people. I want to tell you that we can live so close to Jesus that when we go down from the mountain even to deal with contentious people, we can do that with shining faces if we keep our pronouns straight.

After reminding me of the story of Moses, Papa said, "There is nothing you can do at Indian Springs; you must keep your pronouns straight." He added, "Don't go forward thinking you can do anything for God. You are a carrier of His presence, and if anything is accomplished, He will have to do it. He alone is able to do the work." That was a freeing thought and has been a life saving word for me. You and I have to concentrate on loving Him, living in Him, enjoying Him, and being a carrier of His presence.

Do you remember the last time I was able to be at CTTF? There was a big crowd, and I sat up on the platform and thought, I can't do this! I said, "Father, I don't think I can do this."

Then He said, "Well, Bethie, do you remember Balaam's Donkey?"

And I said, "Yeah."

He replied, "I spoke through a donkey before, and I can do it again."

I thought, "Yes, You did." So that was helpful. I actually made it up to the podium; then I said, "Father, I really don't think I can do it."

He responded, "Who carried My presence to Jerusalem?"

I said, "A donkey."

He said, "Do you think the donkey ever thought, 'I wonder how I'm looking? Is my tail straight? Is my fur going the right direction?'" No, the people didn't even notice the donkey. All they saw was Jesus. And he carried the presence of Jesus into Jerusalem. That has been the second most freeing thing.

When I got home, I went to Drug Mart and bought a little donkey. He sits where I can see him by my bed. He's the funniest little donkey. You can't get a cute donkey, but about every day I pat his little bottom and say, "Simply today all we have to do is carry His presence." It's not about you; it's not about me; it's about Jesus. We must keep our pronouns straight as we go home.

Pay close attention to where God is working and the people He puts into our lives. He can give us heart eyes to see where He is actually working, and it will be with people or situations we don't expect. Someone may snuggle up close and want to carry on a conversation. God can make us so people oriented that we are not "my agenda" people. He can change even our orientation so that we are not driven by our tasks or schedules. When we nestle into Him and keep our pronouns straight, we are carriers of the presence of Jesus even in our homes. We begin to see the sanctity of our washing machine, the sanctity of doing dishes, setting the table, or caring for a loved one who is sick or raising children for God. He is longing for us to raise children for Jesus Christ, to be there for children, teenagers, and young adults, and to be their intercessors. If you are not a mother or grandmother by natural causes, God wants to give you spiritual children so the world is forever different because you lived. He wants us to be disciple makers beginning with those at our own gate.

Jesus comes when we keep our pronouns straight. Let God reorient us so that we no longer think about me, myself, and I, and how fulfilled I am. There is joy even in cancer, radiation, and chemo. He can sanctify those places we don't want to go. He goes with us. He will do the work if we are carriers of His presence and keep our pronouns straight.

Next Papa said, "Bethie, good intentions do not accomplish the work of God even as noble as your good intentions are." He took me to 1 Chronicles 13-15 with a story about David's good intentions. David had just been crowned king after that awful struggle with Saul. He had been faithful as a man of God and immediately wanted to get the Ark of God back to Jerusalem. The Ark had been neglected during the reign of Saul after the Philistines had captured it. David had a good idea to get the Ark of God back to the center of the nation. That's what God is longing for us to do today—to get Him back as the center of our nation.

Weep, wail, and mourn until you are not only saved but also filled with the Spirit; then wail and mourn until God can pour out His Spirit on our nation. But how do we get the Ark of God back into our nation? How do we get the presence of Jesus not only back into our nation, but into us—and into our families, our marriages, our churches, and our communities? It will not be done with good intentions. It has to be done God's way.

David didn't inquire of the Lord. He had a good idea, but he did it his way instead of God's way. Watch those pronouns! He decided to have the Ark of God carried on a new cart and brought from Abinadab's house where it had been for twenty years. Uzza and Ahio drove the cart. When they came to Chidon's threshing floor, the oxen stumbled, and Uzza put out his hand to hold the Ark. Uzza died because his hand touched the Ark.[4] After Uzza died, David, now afraid, took the Ark to the house of Obed-edom of Gath rather than to Jerusalem.

When you and I try to do God's work in our own strength with our pronouns all mixed up, it becomes all about me, and it always brings death. How do we get the presence of Jesus back? It will not be with good intentions. Good intentions do not accomplish the will of God. The only way is by waiting upon God; out of this intimacy and by inquiring of Him about the big and little things is He able to accomplish His work. Then He gets the glory, and we know it is not in us; it is in Him.

You say, "I want to bring the Ark back home to my family so they recognize the presence of Jesus and what He has done in my life."

God says, "You cannot do it in your own strength; you have to inquire of Me." All hell will break through on those who have made decisions for God, but all power is given through Jesus!

When the Philistines heard that David had been crowned King of Israel, they came to capture him, but David was beginning to learn the ways of God. When the Philistines arrived and made a raid on the valley, David didn't do what he did before in His own strength. This time he inquired of the Lord, "Shall I go up against the Philistines? Will You deliver them into my hand?"

The Lord said, "Go up, for I will deliver them into your hand."[5]

So David's troops defeated the Philistines because He had gotten instructions from the Lord. When you get home and the temptations come, all you have to say is, "Jesus, what do you want to do about this?"

Then the Philistines came again and made another raid on the valley. When you go through one battle, you may think the enemy will quit for a while; however, he shows up again. That's why you must daily inquire of the Lord.

Once again David asked God what to do. This time God's instructions were very specific: "You shall not go up after them; circle around them, and come upon them in front of the mulberry trees. And it shall be, when you hear a sound of marching in the tops of the mulberry trees, then you shall go out to battle, for God has gone out before you to strike the camp of the Philistines."[6]

David did what the Lord commanded and struck down the Philistine army. He didn't do it in his own strength. When you and I go out, we do not have to be afraid, but we do have to keep our pronouns straight and inquire of the Lord. It is living the life of continual intercession, keeping continuous conversation with Jesus. "Jesus, what's on Your heart about this situation? What's on Your heart for my neighbor?"

My mother told me the sweetest story. One day Jesus laid a friend named Ruthie on a busy little lady's heart, and she took Ruthie to lunch. It was an encouragement to Ruthie who was going through a hard time. When she went home, she decided to take some of their fresh harvested maple syrup to Ruthie. She put it on the table by the front door to remind her, but she didn't carry out her good intentions right away. Then guests came, so she put the syrup out of the way in the closet by the door. Life got busy, and she forgot.

Has that ever happened to you? Your heart is right, and you haven't moved into the flesh. You've kept your pronouns straight. You've inquired of the Lord, but He has kept you quite busy, and you haven't had time to finish what He wanted you to do.

A month later, the busy little lady went to the closet for her umbrella, and, behold, there was the syrup. She decided to take the syrup right then to Ruthie. When she got to the door, Ruthie was overjoyed and burst into tears, "Today is my birthday! My husband forgot; my children forgot; my mother forgot, but you are the only one who remembered." The friend had no idea it was Ruthie's birthday, but Jesus did! He knows the motives of our heart. Even when things don't seem quite good enough, He can do a greater good fulfilling a more beautiful purpose even down to maple syrup on a women's birthday. He is the kindest Jesus. If you do not know Him today, I pray that you will just fall in love with Jesus, and let Him fill you so that you just slosh over with Him. It's not overwork; it's overflow. It is a sweet love adventure with Jesus.

Keep your pronouns straight; inquire of the Lord; and live in a constant state of His presence. Jesus lived in that intimacy with the Father. He is our Keeper God. He can keep us pure and shining.

Jude, in the book of the Bible just before Revelation, said he was a bondservant of Jesus. If you and I are His bondservant, we belong to Him 100 percent. Jude was writing to believers, to those who had been called, sanctified by God the Father, and kept in Jesus Christ.[7] He can keep us; He makes us holy. "Now may the God of peace Himself sanctify you completely; and may your whole spirit, soul, and body be preserved blameless at the coming of our Lord Jesus Christ. He who calls you is faithful, who also will do it."[8] We are preserved in Jesus Christ and kept in Jesus Christ and out of that relationship mercy, peace, and love overflow out of you and out of me.[9]

Jesus wants to come and keep us because He is a Keeper God. Jude gives a warning to watch out for those who would try to lead you astray—those who do not believe that Jesus is Lord. They are not to be your best friends. You are to give them to Jesus and ask Jesus for friends that have a passion for Him so you can get your feet on the ground.

Jude also warned to watch out for unbelief because, even though God led the people out of Egypt, they didn't make it into the Promised Land since they didn't trust God.[10] Watch out for unbelief as you go home. It's one thing to believe Him in your head and another to consciously put your hand up and say, "Jesus, I choose to trust You even in this." Unbelief can turn us away. Unholy associations can turn us away. Immorality can turn us away. As you spend time in the Word and with Jesus, there will be an abhorrence of evil and a clinging to good. Be careful to guard your heart and mind. The only way any of us—men, women, children, or teenagers—can stay pure is by the power of the Holy Spirit. Do not lose your faith like Sodom and Gomorrah.[11] He can keep your heart pure if you let Him.

Jesus wants to come and make us a holy people and set us free. Why? Because there is a watching world! Every one of us has a different set of connections and relationships, and we are called to be carriers of His presence, to shine forth His glory. You know what so often happens? If we don't keep our hearts stayed in Jesus so He is at home in our heart, we will lose the reality of who He is. Then when a lost world looks at us, they will see clouds with no water instead of clouds that should bring water. We will be like autumn trees that should bring delicious fruit but are dead with no hope of fruit.[12]

There's no hope of anyone finding Jesus when you and I give a blurry picture of who He is. If we are not clean, we have profaned His name, and the world knows it even if we delude ourselves. We become likes waves of the sea that, instead of flowing over with Jesus, bring shame. You know, ladies, the saddest one to me is that when we fail to let Jesus keep us, which He longs to do if we let Him, we become like wandering stars for whom is reserved the blackness of darkness forever.[13]

We never know who is watching us, and when they look at our lives, they need to see the transforming power of Jesus. When they are looking for hope, we have nothing to give them if we are separated from the life of God by our sin. We are the book the world reads. We need to let Jesus fill us so full of Himself that we overflow with His glory. We want to go home and sparkle and shine wherever we are, and we can keep on shining. The end of Jude is beautiful. He closes with this affirmation: "Now to Him who is able to keep you from stumbling, and to present you faultless before the presence of His glory with exceeding joy, to God our Savior, who alone is wise, be glory and majesty, dominion and power, both now and forever."[14]

Oh, what would happen if you and I would become the fellowship of the shining faces? Will you begin to seek Him every single day and throughout the day and become women of the Word?

You know, David didn't know how to bring the Ark back to Jerusalem until he read the Scripture and found out there were clear directions in the Word as to how to transport it. He hadn't read his Bible enough to know it was to be carried by the priests and Levites who were to be sanctified holy before they ever touched the Ark of God. Then the Ark was to be carried not on a pickup truck—new as it might have been—but on the shoulders of the people of God.

This time David summoned the priests and called for the leaders of the Levite families to purify themselves so they could bring the Ark to the place he had prepared. He acknowledged that the first time they had failed to ask God how to move it properly. "So the priests and the Levites purified themselves in order to bring the Ark of the LORD, the God of Israel, to Jerusalem. Then the Levites carried the Ark of God on their shoulders with its carrying poles, just as the LORD had instructed Moses."[15]

You and I cannot do the work of God or be the people of God unless God has made us clean—every whit. Are there any hidden places in your soul? Will you say, "Jesus, come and set me free from myself?" This is the moment of all moments.

I met a lady in Mississippi who said, "I need to talk to you right now!" When we stepped outside, she asked, "Do you think God is big enough to set me free from myself?" Then she added, "I am so sick of me. I'm even sick of my own inner conversations. They are just all about me."

"Honey," I said, "I challenge you to dare Him to change your introspection and self love." We sat on the porch, and God came and set her free. I noticed when we got up her face was glowing. It's God's secret. It's the secret of the shining face. When He comes and sets us free, the home of our heart is His. So we no longer are into me, myself, and I, and what's in it for me, and "No, I deserve better than this!" Even when you have a blood transfusion and you're a little bit loopy, do you know who comes out? Jesus! It's the sweetest thing. I invite you today to let Jesus come and set you free and keep you free!

Years ago, we were at Indian Springs in a house with thirty-two in-laws. We had a two-year-old toddler who would wake up early and awaken everyone just being a little boy. So as soon as Billy would wake early in the morning, I would put him in the stroller with Cheerios and apple juice and push him around the campground. The only thing going on at a holiness camp meeting early in the morning is the prayer meeting, and I didn't go to early morning prayer meetings at that time in my life. The first day as I was pushing the stroller and got to the back of the tabernacle, I suddenly heard this little woman at the altar pray, "Oh, Jesus, would You fill us so full of You today that we just slosh all over with Jesus?"

So the next morning I put Billy in the stroller again and prayed, "Jesus, don't let that lady pray yet. Wait for me! Wait for me until I get there."

This time I didn't go to the back; I went closer scouting out the lady. Then I saw her. She began to pray,

"Oh, fill us so full of You, Jesus, that we are just like fresh ripe peaches, and when people walk by, they want to taste the goodness of that peach."

Later I said to my friend Joy, "You've got to go to prayer meeting with me tomorrow morning."

She said, "Bethie, why would I do that?"

I said, "You've got to go hear this lady pray. She doesn't just know about God. She knows God."

The passion of her soul was Jesus, and I actually wanted to make Jesus the passion of my soul, but at that moment I just didn't know how.

The next morning I had a plan. We got Billy up, and I said, "We will see where she sits, and you get on the right; I will get on the left, and when she sloshes over, we will be in the overflow." It was like Billy's divine assignment; there he sat as good as gold. Sure enough, when the little lady prayed, the overflow just sloshed all over us. Afterwards we introduced ourselves and said, "How do you know Him like that?"

She shared that she had married her childhood sweetheart when she was very young. They had a baby; then her sweetheart started to drink and became an alcoholic, and she didn't know what to do. Someone shared Jesus with her, and she said, "I took all the pain, all the hopes and dreams, and I gave Him all of me for all of Him. When I did that, He became the true husband of my heart. And I claimed Isaiah 54:13 for my children: 'All your children shall be taught by the Lord, and great shall be the peace of your children'" (NKJV).

She continued, "I inquired of the Lord what to do next. Sometimes we were separated. I cleaned houses and taught school, but at every point, there was Jesus. See this Bible, the tear marks, they are my tears that only Jesus knows. Jesus, Jesus, Jesus has met me every step of the way."

I knew her husband; I knew he loved Jesus as much as she did. He also overflowed with Jesus. God had heard and answered her prayers. She kept her pronouns straight and kept inquiring of the Lord.

Later she was diagnosed with leukemia, but she continued coming to camp meeting. One year she said, "I don't know if I will be here next year."

She went home and had to have surgery. They knocked her out, and as they were pushing her on the gurney, someone commented that she was very religious. She sat up and said, "No, it's not religion; it's Jesus." Even in her unconscious state, she preached Jesus, and at her celebration service, nine people found Jesus Christ.

Now unto Him who is able to keep you and me from falling and to present you and me faultless before the presence of His glory—with stress, with disappointment, with heartbreak, with joy, with exceeding great joy—To God our Savior who alone is wise be glory and majesty, dominion and power, both now and forever. Amen[16]

Those who are wise will shine as bright as the sky, and those who lead many to righteousness will shine like the stars forever (Daniel 12:3).

My Chains Are Gone

CTTF Attendees

Set Free

Fear had become a chain of bondage for me. I had been releasing links of this chain daily, but it wasn't until CTTF that I truly felt free and began to enjoy resting in Him, trusting Him completely. Now, when fear arises, I place it in Jesus' lap and literally speak out loud, "I will trust you Lord!" Since CTTF, God has taken me on an incredible journey of learning to trust Him more and more. Most recently, the Lord had my husband and me step out completely in faith, leaving a life of comfort, familiarity, and security to a journey of trusting Him, one day at a time and, in some cases, one hour at a time.

Revived

At the conference, God reaffirmed that although he has freed me from the paralyzing chains of self-consciousness, he still loves me when I retreat to behaving like the introvert I am. I was especially strengthened by seeing Jesus shining through the different personalities who make up the team and through those who testified to the chains He has broken in their lives and the lies of the enemy they will no longer believe. Their openness is such a priceless witness to what God can do in anyone's life when He is allowed to shine through! Each one is unique and reflects him in a special way. This year He revived me and especially renewed my call to be an intercessor.

Released

This was my first time to the conference, and I am so thankful that God allowed me to come. I will never forget the healing service. What a sweet release of emotional abuse, shame, and guilt of over twenty-five years. Although I love Jesus, I carried so much baggage I could never move forward with the joy I so longed for in Christ. The accuser, the father of all lies, had me bound in chains of not forgiving myself even though Christ had forgiven me. What a heavy burden I had carried until those chains were broken on Friday. Praise God that He broke every chain. No longer will I believe the lies of the devil. When he comes to remind me, and I know he will, I will just remind him of that Friday in October when freedom came because Christ broke every chain.

Centered

Nashville was my first CTTF conference; at that time, God used the interactive prayer room to heal my childhood memories. At the Grove City and Olivet conferences, God brought healing of my teen years and an abusive time. The next year, the chain of being a people pleaser and the bondage that comes from failing were taken off! God has come through loud and clear that all I need to do is keep Him at the center of my life, read the Word and worship Him, and He will flow through me. What a relief! It's all about keeping the pronouns straight! Thank you for a time to enjoy God's presence and the privilege of seeing Him at work in all of our lives! God be praised!

Lifted

I came into the conference bitter, angry, hopeless, and lost. I was not in a good place in my life and didn't think this conference was going to impact me. In fact I almost didn't even come. But through the music, the speakers, and God's presence, I was forever changed. I cried, confessed, gave my chains to Jesus, and had a weight lifted off me. I realized I was lying to myself and putting on an act for a few hours a week, but I wasn't following the Lord or giving him a chance to fill me with the Holy Spirit. My life will never be the same; I will be a better person, and most importantly, Jesus will call me His child on Judgment Day.

Filled

God showed me that my thoughts of rejection, failure, and shame were not sinful but had been planted by the enemy. God delivered me from these chains, and now I am free to overcome these lies through the power of His Spirit in me. God can also deliver me from my self-centeredness so I can serve my family and others. I want to be so filled with Jesus that He sloshes out, but I can't do that without the power of God's presence in my life. God met me at the CTTF simulcast. It was the spiritual renewal I needed to get back on track and put God first in my life.

Accepted

When I came for the first time last year, God healed some generational wounds passed down through my relationship with my mom who suffered from an inferiority complex and had trouble accepting people's, and probably God's, love for her. What spoke to me most last year besides the healing service itself was the song "God Declares Who I Am."

Praising

Come to the Fire was a beautiful movement of God! Our busload of fifty-six ladies continued to praise God all the way home. We had more women in their twenties through forties than we did older women. We all were rejoicing and praising God.

Growing

Come to the Fire was indescribable really. My chains are gone, and I feel lighter, free, and closer to our Lord. I didn't know that my relationship could grow this much more in such a short time. Through the verses on the altars, I know that He was speaking to me! It brought tears of great joy!

Leaning

The healing session was powerful. Carolyn Johnson began the session by giving us a card that stated "Broken things in my life." She referenced Colossians 1:13, 14: "For he has rescued us from the dominion of darkness and brought us into the kingdom of the Son he loves, in whom we have redemption, the forgiveness of sins."

Then we came to a time of confession from James 5:16: "Therefore confess your sins to each other and pray for each other so that you may be healed."

As we prayed, the big question on the card that I felt the Lord showing me was, "Do I want to be well?" In my heart I spoke, "Yes, Yes, Yes, I do, Lord." My actions and behavior had created fear and anxiety, a roller coaster ride I was ready to end.

The next question was, "What do I hear from God?"

I heard that I deserve the freedom of His gift to release my burdens. He said, "Take it from Me, Child. It is My gift to you." But, was I ready?

The last question on the card was, "What do I want to say to God?"

I wrote, "I am willing to receive Your gift and Your will for me. I open the door for Your healing."

As we were praying in groups, the prayer team placed scriptures at the altar for each of us to pick up. I was praying with a sister, so a friend picked up a verse for me. It read, "'For I know the plans I have for you,' declares the Lord, 'plans to prosper you and not to harm you, plans to give you hope and a future'" (Jeremiah 29:11 NIV).

You see one of my greatest burdens was financial stress, and with that Scripture confirmation, I have been able to be patient and trust. When the fear comes in, I now give it right back to Him. I'm learning to trust His decisions for me and lean on Him!

Part IX

Embrace the Cross

Aletha Hinthorn

Then he said to them all: "If anyone would come after me, he must deny himself and take up his cross daily and follow me" (Luke 9:23 Berean Study Bible).

Because of the joy set before Him, Jesus endured the cross and disregarded its disgrace. There is great joy for us, too, when we also take up our cross and follow Him. He who invites us to deny ourselves also enables us to embrace the cross He has lovingly chosen for us.

The message of the cross is foolishness to those who are headed for destruction! But we who are being saved know it is the very power of God (I Corinthians 1:18).

Chapter 17

Embrace the Cross with Confident Hope

Patsy Lewis

I pray that your hearts will be flooded with light so that you can understand the confident hope he has given to those he called—his holy people who are his rich and glorious inheritance (Ephesians 1:18).

When we were in Grove City in June 2014 to pray and plan with the local team of volunteers, I attended the Wednesday evening prayer meeting. Pastor Fuller had the people circle around to pray for me. He asked me to speak and give a report; then I knelt, and several knelt beside me. Then others gathered around—everyone who was there—and all voices were raised in crying out prayers. I believe there were more men than women ages probably twenties through eighties—and as they prayed, tears began to fall on my arms and hands! Indescribable! What happens at the location before a conference greatly affects what happens during Come to the Fire. I left that prayer meeting with confident hope, anticipating what God had in store as women from around the nation and beyond embraced the cross and put their hope in the victorious Jesus, our Living Hope!

As I was preparing for the Friday morning session, I knew the theme was to be "Embrace the Cross with Confident Hope," and God gave me the names of several ladies to invite to speak in that session.

• Ruth Chandler shared the confident hope of eternal life when we open our heart's door to Jesus, and she gave us a plan for presenting the Good News to others—to embrace the cross for salvation.

• Jenny Jordan read her story giving encouragement to never give up praying for lost loved ones and to keep hope alive that they will one day embrace the cross.

• Pam Enderby gave an example of how God interweaves our obedience to bring hoped for results and the joy of leading others to embrace the cross.

• Dorinda Biggs made it clear through her testimony that we can have confident hope and lift praises to the great I AM in the midst of life's trauma.

• Sonia Samayoa delivered the message that our confident hope is anchored in an intimate love relationship with Jesus.

• Stephanie Hogan proclaimed the Word that a victorious Christian life is possible through complete surrender—"All of me for all of Him." He is our Living Hope!

Praise be to the God and Father of our Lord Jesus Christ! In his great mercy he has given us new birth into a living hope through the resurrection of Jesus from the dead, and into an inheritance that can never perish, spoil or fade. This inheritance is kept in heaven for you (I Peter 1:3-4 NIV).

Chapter 18

Open the Door of Your Heart

Ruth Chandler[1]

For God loved the world so much that he gave his one and only Son, so that everyone who believes in him will not perish but have eternal life (John 3:16).

My late husband, Robert Maner, was a pastor for fifty years; then he semi-retired to be the people pastor on staff of a new congregation. They soon learned that if Bob was asked to pray for someone, he took it very seriously.

Dorothy, a lady in our church, asked Bob to pray for her son-in-law, Bob Banks. He had never been to our church though his wife, Judy, and his mother-in-law were life long, active members. Bob Banks had just discovered he had cancer. My husband prayed for him daily. One Sunday Dorothy asked my husband if he would visit Bob Banks at his home. She said he wasn't feeling well though the cancer had been discovered early, and the doctor felt that he would be fine.

At breakfast on Monday, Bob said he felt impressed to go see Bob Banks that day. He asked if I would stay home and pray while he made the visit. We had never met the man but had been told that he was self-sufficient and didn't feel he needed God. After meeting him, my husband described him as a man's man. Mr. Banks was career Army and had served in Vietnam twice, earning a purple heart for valor both times.

Judy took Bob to the bedroom where she introduced him as Pastor Bob and left. He said it was an awkward moment, but he told Bob Banks that he had been praying for him and that he understood he had always been able to handle life by himself. My husband commented that this might be one problem he needed help with and gave him a Heart's Door card. He explained that it was a picture depicting Revelation 3:20 where Jesus said, "Here I am! I stand at the door and knock. If anyone hears my voice and opens the door, I will come in and eat with him, and he with me."[1]

Bob explained that the arches over the door represent our heart. The window is dark within. The Bible says we have all sinned. Jesus is illuminated in the painting because He is the light of the world, and when He comes into our heart, He drives out the darkness. The bushes in the picture have grown half way up the door, which tells us that Jesus is patient. He waits for us to open the door and invite Him in. At this point, my husband asked Bob Banks, "Do you think Jesus is knocking at your heart's door?"

Bob Banks said emphatically, "No."

Most would have stopped there. I am afraid I would have, but my husband felt compelled to continue. He said, "Listen! Listen real good; don't you hear him?" There was a sniffle, and a tear made its way down Bob Banks' cheek. The Holy Spirit was working! My husband was able to lead Bob Banks to the Lord. The spiritual birth certificate was filled out on the back of the card with Bob Banks' name, the date, and Bob Maner as witness.

Bob Banks called for Judy and Dorothy and said, "Jesus just saved me." What rejoicing there was in the house!

The following day on Tuesday, Bob Banks had a doctor's appointment. After a brief examination, the doctor sadly said, "I am so sorry. There is nothing we can do for you. You probably have about six weeks to live."

Judy burst into tears. Bob pulled out the Heart's Door card he had carried in his shirt pocket, patted Judy on the knee, and said, "It's going to be okay."

On Wednesday my husband went to visit with Bob Banks. He asked to be baptized, and they made arrangements for Friday. Bob baptized him at home with his wife and mother-in-law watching. Again, there was rejoicing in the house!

The next afternoon Judy called and asked us to come. Bob Banks had just passed away. What a shock! He didn't have six weeks; he didn't even have six days. We got to the house before the hearse picked him up. Family, friends and neighbors had gathered. Judy asked my husband if he would lead a victory march. He took Judy's arm, and we all walked with Bob Banks from the house to the hearse singing "Amazing Grace." What an incredible journey that was! Heaven was very near.

Judy said, "Pastor Bob, at the funeral, just tell Bob's story. People have to hear." That's what Bob did; he told the story. Judy placed the Heart's Door card in her husband's hand, and he was buried holding it.

What an honor it was for me to have a small part in this salvation story! Our job as Christians is to tell others about Jesus.

This story was told on Friday morning at Come to the Fire 2014. Approximately 2,500 ladies received a Heart's Door card and learned to share Jesus. They were also given an *I Am Second* New Testament. Emails after the conference told of women who had used the card and their New Testaments to tell others about Jesus.

Since that time I have been asked on numerous occasions to share a salvation story and teach the Heart's Door card. Jennifer, a youth pastor who had never led anyone to Jesus, went home after learning to use the Heart's Door card at a District Ladies' Day on Saturday and led two of her youth to the Lord the following Wednesday night. One teen brought a younger brother so Jennifer could help tell him about Jesus, and he was saved. The youth group continues to grow, and many have asked Jesus into their heart.

At Jennifer's wedding shower, I was asked to share the Heart's Door card; then each table practiced with the person sitting next to them. Two people asked Jesus to come into their hearts for real as they practiced at the wedding shower!

Donna learned to use the Heart's Door card at a women's brunch. She had visited in the local prison twice a month for thirty-two years but did not know how to lead anyone to the Lord. After the brunch she told me she thought she could do this, referring to sharing the card. In seven months she has helped 109 ladies ask Jesus to come into their hearts!

Another friend, Annetta, an ordained elder, has begun a jail ministry in her town, and at her first meeting, two ladies came to know Jesus and two recommitted their lives to Him. Earlier, Annetta had led two elderly ladies in her church to the Lord using the Heart's Door card. Both have since gone to be with Jesus.

Our District Women's Retreat is fashioned after Come to the Fire. This fall at our retreat with Dr. Carolyn Johnson, we focused on prayer and evangelism. A number of ladies told salvation stories, and two hundred women were trained to use the Heart's Door card to share Jesus. Each lady went home with several cards and a MY HOPE video donated by the Billy Graham Evangelistic Association to help them share Jesus. I have no salvation numbers from the retreat, but the printer who produces the card has had a number of requests for more cards. This is a great tool to use to tell others about Jesus. It's easy to remember and a good visual. Even children can use it to tell their friends about Jesus.

When Patsy Lewis asked me to share Bob Banks' salvation story and the Heart's Door card at Come to the Fire, who could have imagined that God would take those few moments to give me renewed courage and open doors for opportunities to teach others to share Jesus. I am so grateful that over the years there have been special times of spiritual challenge and growth because of CTTF. I will forever be different because of it.

Jesus told his disciples, "I have been given all authority in heaven, and on earth. Therefore, go and make disciples of all the nations, baptizing them in the name of the Father and the Son and the Holy Spirit. Teach these new disciples to obey all the commands I have given you. And be sure of this: I am with you, always, even to the end of the age" (Matthew 28:18-20).

Chapter 19

Jenny's Story

Story read by Jenny at Come to the Fire 2014

Once you were like sheep who wandered away. But now you have turned to your Shepherd, the Guardian of your souls (I Peter 2:25).

Jenny, a classical musician, was headed toward Juilliard School of Music, but her life choices led her down a totally different path of extreme destruction, and now she lives with great remorse over her years of sin and the scars that remain. This talented girl was raised in church, knew about Jesus all her life, and had praying parents and grandparents. She called on Jesus many times, but left her place of prayer to make selfish, unwise decisions.

Her sad story included unwanted pregnancies, abortions, drugs, theft, arrests, mental illness, eating disorders, multiple divorces, numerous suicide attempts, and, in her own words, demons of evil within and without. Sadly, she was a slave to sin, a shell of a person, trying in her own power to keep the law, please her parents, be a good girl, and break the bondages, but was living in a Romans 7 state—struggling with sin, defeated for years.

Today she is living in an Easter world, resurrected to new life in Christ—forgiven, obedient out of love, victorious, maturing in her Christian walk, and joyfully sharing her faith. Romans 8 is her testimony! Jenny is now living in freedom because she has confessed, repented, turned from sin and been forgiven, cleansed, and reconciled to God. She is being discipled through Christian counseling, accountability partners, group Bible studies, daily obedience, her pastor's Biblical teaching, replacing lies of the enemy with truth from God's word, reading inspirational literature, sharing her story, calling on the name of the Lord in prayer, listening, and following His call!

Jenny radiates Jesus even in the midst of today's trials. Among other difficulties, she is facing major cancer surgery. She is aware that God has spared her life many times, and she will have opportunities to share her joy and hope with people she otherwise would never have met. Jenny's joy inspires me. She is a living example of one being dead to sin yet now very much alive by the power of the resurrected Jesus![2]

He personally carried our sins in his body on the cross so that we can be dead to sin and live for what is right. By his wounds you are healed (I Peter 2:24).

Chapter 20

Sharing the Word

Pam Enderby
Story Told Spontaneously at Come to the Fire 2014

For the word of God is alive and powerful. It is sharper than the sharpest two-edged sword, cutting between soul and spirit, between joint and marrow. It exposes our innermost thoughts and desires (Hebrews 4:12).

When I learned Ruth Chandler would be presenting how to share your faith at Come to the Fire 2014, I thought, wouldn't it be wonderful for each attendee to receive a free New Testament! The Lord of the harvest provided His tools. MyFreeBible.org[1] freely shipped 2,000 New Testaments to Grove City. Combined with the salvation story that Ruth told the conference attendees about Bob Banks, they returned home equipped to share their faith!

A few days before the Grove City Come to the Fire, a friend shared the following interesting witnessing story with me:

While eating lunch at Olive Garden, Mike and Dale discussed their mission outreach to Sudan and Nepal.

Little did they realize the Lord had planted them, at that specific time, for another outreach in Olathe, Kansas.

Mike and Dale exchanged small talk with Susie,[2] their waitress. They learned she was a University of Kansas student commuting back and forth to work. While Susie lingered at their table, Mike sensed the Holy Spirit prompt him to talk to her about Jesus. The enemy immediately countered. "She's taking a biology class; she thinks creation is nonsense."

Mike recognized Satan's voice trying to discourage him. Should he back off and ignore the Spirit's prompting? He might get ridiculed talking about Jesus. Mike rebuked the enemy and went on.

"Susie, I'm going to ask you a question."

"OK," she said.

"Susie, have you ever experienced the love of Jesus?"

"No, I haven't, but it's odd you would ask me." Susie reached down in her apron and pulled out a light blue New Testament. "You know, the table I waited on right before you—well, they left this for me with a tip. Then you asked me if I've ever experienced the love of Jesus."

Dale chimed in, and with the help of the Holy Spirit, he explained to Susie about Jesus' love. The beautiful gospel message made sense to Susie, and she prayed right there in the Olive Garden to give her life to Jesus.

Often we never know how God will use our obedience to His promptings—leaving a Bible for a waitress or offering some other act of kindness. This time, the unknown became known.

At church that evening, Mike shared this amazing story with his business partner. His partner rejoiced and immediately called his elderly parents because they often leave well-prayed over New Testaments in restaurants. Could they possibly be the ones responsible for Susie's salvation? Sure enough! They had been at the Olive

Garden earlier that day. June, his mother, had left the New Testament on the table with a generous tip.

The Lord continued to weave His amazing work. Kara[3], who also attended Dale and Mike's church, worked with Susie at the same Olive Garden. When Kara heard about Susie's salvation she connected with Susie and offered to disciple her.

When Holy Spirit promptings come, we're presented with a choice. Do we take a risk and act on what we've heard? Or ignore His gentle nudge? Let's not allow excuses to rob us of the indescribable joy of sharing Jesus' love. Here's a helpful hint. Begin to sincerely pray this simple prayer: "Lord, set my heart ablaze with your love for the lost." Just pray. The Holy Spirit will change your heart. Someday you may be the one offering a New Testament or sharing the love of Jesus with someone in a restaurant, the mall, or at the grocery store!

But you will receive power when the Holy Spirit comes upon you. And you will be my witnesses, telling people about me everywhere—in Jerusalem, throughout Judea, in Samaria, and to the ends of the earth (Acts 1:8).

Chapter 21

Lament and Praise

Dorinda Biggs[1]

I will praise the LORD *at all times. I will constantly speak his praises (Psalm 34:1).*

I first participated in the Come to the Fire worship team in 2008. In 2010 Kim McLean invited several of us to attend a Come to the Fire songwriting retreat to write new songs of praise for the next conference. While I worked on "The Great I Am" with a couple teammates, I had no idea how that song would become my battle cry.

Over the past few years since that song was written, I have experienced a lot of painful circumstances—so many that at times I thought I would not be able to catch my breath. Each one was covered in prayer, and yet all these happenings were overwhelming to the fullest extent. Loss after loss after loss of loved ones, illnesses that cripple and wound, behavioral issues that isolate, prideful words that gouge, devastating news left and right. In all these things, resentment and disdain have been tempting because, frankly, people I love have caused most of the painful circumstances in my life.

I've thought about how I could have done things differently—how others could have done things differently—not to mention all the hot, tear-filled "whys." I know this life is not free of pain, disappointment, grief, or fear, and I am instructed to count all those things joy (James 1:2-8).

When I look at I Corinthians 10:13, I think of all the things that have tempted me over this time. Life has been more than I felt I could bear these past years. It has been a stripping of all I thought was secure in my life, only to find that the One who has been there all along has never left my side. I do not believe God caused these things to happen. My real mystery is grasping God's view of it all and knowing that He allowed these things to happen; after all, I believed and trusted Him before all this!

One thing He promised me in a time of desperate prayer is that He would not let my family or me come to ruin. Temptation has come to flee, to seclude, to hate, to isolate, to self-preserve, to loathe, to treat with something other than God. It's truly been a battle! My battle weapons have been worshipping Him, praising Him, praying over it and under it, surrendering, reading and praying the Word!

I am praising Him today for His presence, for His love, for His mercy and grace, for His unending joy that is always available, for His healing, His strength and His shelter. I praise Him for His sacrifice, His friendship, His readiness and boldness. I praise Him for the battles that bring me closer to Him and show His power and glory. I praise Him for the way He speaks and the quietness of His voice. Praise You, Father, for never leaving my side and for the redemption You promise. Amen.

Song: "The Great I Am"

We enter the battle praising You, Lord of Heaven's Army.

We fight the battle praising You, Lord of Heaven's Army.

    The great I Am!
    The great I Am!
    The great I Am!

Jesus, You're the Prince of Peace, King of kings, Almighty God,

    Alpha, Omega, the beginning and end,

    Messiah, You're the Living God, Emmanuel, Ancient of Days,

    Savior, Redeemer, who is the Lamb.

    Jesus! Word of God!
    Jesus! Cornerstone!
    Jesus! Conqueror! We lift You up!

We enter the battle praising You, Lord of Heaven's Army.

We fight the battle praising You, Lord of Heaven's Army.

    The great I Am!
    The great I Am!
    The great I Am!

I will boast only in the LORD; let all who are helpless take heart. Come, let us tell of the LORD's greatness; let us exalt his name together (Psalm 34:2-3).

Chapter 22

Intimacy with God

Sonia Samayoa[1]

Jesus replied, "You must love the LORD *your God with all your heart, all your soul, and all your mind. This is the first and greatest commandment" (Matthew 22:37-38).*

Like many of you, I enjoyed praying with my children before bed when they were young. One night, it was four-year-old Isaac's turn. He used to pray for our family, our neighbors, our neighbors' pets and church members—by name! So, you had to be seated comfortably because he would take his time! That special night, Isaac was very joyful, and at the end of his prayer he said, "Lord, I'm so happy and so blessed, and the only thing I want to do is send you a kiss!"

I wanted to tell Isaac, "Sending kisses to Jesus is not part of the prayer." But I didn't say anything.

I went to my bed reflecting on what he had said, and I realized that the relationship between Isaac and Jesus was so close that he believed he could kiss Him. I realized also that I'd never had an expression like that toward Jesus.

My prayers were more informative as if I were giving a report or sending a memo like, "Thank You, Lord, because Your presence was so evident in our worship time;" or "Lord, please heal this person;" or "Please bless our church plans."

I received answers to my prayers, but still my relationship wasn't like Isaac's with Jesus. At some point in my life, I had lost it. So I found a passage that talks to me about this:

"Many will say to me on that day, 'Lord, Lord, did we not prophesy in your name and in your name drive out demons and in your name perform many miracles?' Then I will tell them plainly, 'I never knew you. Away from me, you evil doers!'" (Matthew 7:22-23 NIV)

When I read this passage for the first time I thought, "I want these guys on my team!" They could preach and perform many miracles and drive out demons. Not many can drive out demons. But because they could, they came to give their report just like I did: "We did this; we did that."

The Lord responded to them, "I never knew you."

As a pastor's wife, I have done many things for my Lord. I led worship; I taught Sunday School; I was very involved in missions; and I also cooked tacos for a bunch of people! But at the end, all that really matters is whether or not the Lord knows me.

I love this passage because I discovered that nothing is more important to the Lord than getting to know me through my own words. He is eager to know us! He wants to know everything about me.

In her book *Simply Praying*, Patsy Lewis invites us to "open your heart" to Jesus, so I did.[2] I realized that I share my testimony with everyone except Jesus. He saved me, but I never talked with Him about it again. After several years I wanted to tell him what that day meant to me so I prayed:

"Remember that day, Lord? I was six years old, and I was in my Sunday School class.

"To be honest with You, I don't remember what the lesson was about. The only thing I remember is that I could not wait to invite You to come into my heart. Do You remember, Lord? Do You know me?"

In that moment my room was full of His presence, and He responded to me, "Yes, I know you; you are Mine!" These were the most beautiful words I had ever heard! He enjoys remembering good times with His people because that is what friends do. I started to recall when He called me to His service and joyful times we have had together. Since that day, my way of praying changed.

Probably you spend a good bit of time in a Christian environment or working hard for our Lord, but that means nothing if you don't have a real relationship with Jesus. Today, we need to remember that we must put the Word of God and prayer first before all work that we will perform. There is so much to do for the Lord! Is it not true? But in these opportunities, God warns us about the danger of going before him with hands full of projects successfully performed without having engaged in a personal relationship with Him.

I like to think of God as the doctor who asks me some questions after receiving the results of my exams: "Do you eat well?" "Do you work out?" I'm sure He knows the answers, but Jesus wants me to tell Him everything because that is the way that I will become aware of my situation. He wants to heal me, advise me, comfort me, know me. He wants to have an intimate relationship with me like my son Isaac sending kisses to Him.

My sheep listen to my voice; I know them, and they follow me (John 10:27).

Chapter 23

Embrace Jesus —All of Me for All of Him

Stephanie Hogan[1]

God's Word says to you and me today in Ezekiel 36:25-28: I will sprinkle clean water on you, and you will be clean. Your filth will be washed away, and you will no longer worship idols. And I will give you a new heart, and I will put a new spirit in you. I will take out your stony, stubborn heart and give you a tender, responsive heart. And I will put my Spirit in you so that you will follow my decrees and be careful to obey my regulations...You will be my people and I will be your God."

In I John, chapters 1 and 2, John is telling us what he has seen and heard first hand, and we are hearing his witness to us as he talks about Jesus who is life and light.

"This is the message we heard from Jesus and now declare to you: God is light, and there is no darkness in him at all. So we are lying if we say we have fellowship with God but go on living in spiritual darkness; we are not practicing the truth. But if we are living in the light, as God is in the light, then we have fellowship with each other, and the blood of Jesus cleanses us from all sin. If we claim we have no sin, we are only fooling ourselves and not living in the truth. But if we confess our sins to him, he is faithful and just to forgive us our sins and to cleanse us from all wickedness. If we claim we have not sinned, we are calling God a liar and showing that his word has no place in our hearts. My dear children, I am writing this to you so that you will not sin. But if anyone does sin, we have an advocate who pleads our case before the Father. He is Jesus Christ the one who is truly righteous. He himself is the sacrifice that atones for our sins—and not only our sins, but the sins of all the world."

Prayer

Jesus, Father, Son, and Holy Spirit, God in three persons but one God, thank You that You are here and that You have been talking to our hearts. In this moment, I ask a very dangerous prayer. Will You draw us out of darkness into light, out of hiding into living truth? Would You draw us into the light of Your presence that we would have intimacy and know You and know each other and allow ourselves to be known by You and filled with You? Thank You because that is what You long to do. In Jesus name, amen.

Message

God created Adam and Eve so He could know them and so they could know Him—not just for them to know about God, but to know Him personally like you know family. That's why God created us—for fellowship with Him.

God, who is absolute love, gave Adam and Eve everything they could have wanted. Yet the serpent slithered up to Eve and whispered to her heart, "Does

God really mean what He says? He's holding something back from you. He doesn't really love you." Doubt began to linger in Eve's heart.

Those lies are the same lies the evil one speaks to you and me saying that God doesn't love us, that He's holding something back from us, that He doesn't mean what He says, that we can't trust Him. Eve and Adam chose to turn their back on absolute love. Eve and Adam thought they had a better way; they believed lies. They thought they had to fight for themselves and couldn't trust God. At that time, sin entered the world. Sin separates us from God—meaning we don't trust God or follow His ways and plans. As a result, everyone after Adam and Eve was born with a self nature, a natural bent to do the opposite of what God wants; we don't trust Him.

God knew all of this, and His heart was broken because He is a holy God and cannot be near sin. In His kindness, He created a system so mankind could come and dwell with Him again. This required bringing sacrifices. An animal's blood could be shed making it possible to be made right with God and to come into His presence again. God's people over and over and over again had to sacrifice; blood had to be shed; perfect lambs had to be killed. In His mercy, God created this system of sacrifice because He wanted to be in the center of His people. That system paved the way so that you and I no longer had to be bound by sin, and we could enter into the intimacy of a relationship with Him.

"He was despised and rejected—a man of sorrows, acquainted with deepest grief. We turned our back on him and looked the other way. He was despised, and we did not care" (Isaiah 53:3).

This Scripture is talking about Jesus, the second person of the Trinity, God Himself who is seated at the right hand of the Father making intercession for us.

When the Father sent Jesus to earth, He left the right hand of the Father and was born a baby. God Himself took on flesh and with it all of our limitations and humanity. He lived and walked as we do and was tempted with our temptations. He faced loneliness, grief, despair; He walked in our shoes. He has been where we are; He understands us, and He showed us who God is and what true love really looks like.

We pick up the next verses in Isaiah:

"Yet it was our weaknesses he carried; it was our sorrows that weighed him down....But he was pierced for our rebellion, crushed for our sins. He was beaten so we could be whole. He was whipped so we could be healed. We have left God's path to follow our own. Yet, the LORD laid on him the sins of us all" (Isaiah 53:4-6).

God is absolute, holy love, and He created law and order. He gave His Word as a way to live that hems us into His holy love and keeps us from destruction, death, and decay. When we step outside of His way, we know full well the consequences of those choices.

In the ultimate act of love, Jesus who never sinned took on your sin and mine—and not only yours and mine, but the sins of the whole world. He took them upon Himself. He became the sacrifice for your sins and mine with His shed blood. By confessing and allowing His blood to cover our sins, we become whole. His blood cleanses our sin, heals our wounds, makes a way for us to come to our heavenly Father. Jesus' blood is the divine exchange. We give Jesus our sins, pain, guilt, sickness, grief, and He gives us His righteousness, nature, character, holiness. Incredible!

I love how Beth says it: "It's all of me for all of Him." In that moment on the cross, Jesus said, "It is finished." The final sacrifice had been made; the last sacrificial blood had been shed by God Himself.

Some of us can identify with the stories we have heard of how He can give your stony heart a new nature, a heart of flesh. Others of us have grown up in the church, said yes to Him at an early age, and have walked with Him in every way that we know, but still have ways that sin and circumstances creep in.

John Wesley and some of his associates met together and were so hungry to know God and be fully His, fully cleansed, that they would ask each other questions to make sure there was nothing there that did not reflect Jesus. They would ask each other and themselves:

• Am I trying to leave the impression I am something I am not? Am I a hypocrite?

• Am I honest in all my acts and words? Do I exaggerate?

• Do I pass on confidential information? Can I be trusted?

• Am I a slave to anything—friends or work habits?

• Did the Bible live in me today? Am I enjoying prayer?

• Am I defeated in any part of my spiritual walk?

• Am I irritable, touchy?

• How do I spend my spare time?

These aren't questions trying to be scrupulous; they are not self-torture. What they realized is that sin kills. Some of you have walked though situations with self or children or friends who are sick, and you don't just say, "Oh, it's just cancer; get over it; the rest of your body is healthy and whole. Enjoy life; what's the big deal?" We know that cancer kills, and we want every single cell of it out of our body. That is the way with sin. It will eat us alive.

I am afraid that in light of our selfish nature that says, "I want to have my own way," you and I can often create a god that will let us have our own pleasure, have our own selfish way, stay in our weaknesses, or stay hidden. When Adam and Eve sinned, the first thing they did was hide, and they made some pretty pathetic fig leaf coverings. We also find ways to hide from God and each other when we sin and participate in things that separate us from Him—things like what our minds think on—what we allow ourselves to watch. Susannah Wesley told her son John, "Anything that diminishes your affection for God is sin to you." But we can also stay hidden from God in fear, in pain. When life brings us pain, it is hard; we can allow that pain to become our identity, and we hold onto it.

I recall a time in my life when God asked me to release the greatest pain I had ever known. My response was, "Jesus, I don't even get to keep my pain?" No, because He knows that it will destroy us. He offers us new life, and it's so kind of Jesus. God didn't leave Adam and Eve in the shame of being uncovered; He took away their pitiful coverings and gave them appropriate clothing.

You don't have to be afraid of God; He sees every bit of your hurt and pain—every bit of you and your struggle. Remember that He knows the number of the hairs on your head; He loves you intimately.

In Romans 8, Paul talks about it so beautifully; He takes our sin on the cross; He conquers sin, death, hell, and the grave. He sits at the right hand of the Father, and He prays for you and me. He is restored to the right hand of the Father! Jesus invites us to follow Him. He does not want us to live with the filth of sin any longer—or the fake coverings that we make. He died on the cross not only to forgive and cleanse you and me of our sin, but to give us a new nature, a new center, His nature. Peter says He wants to give us His divine nature.[2]

We were created to be filled with the Holy Spirit—filled with all the fullness of God,[3] and the way to enter into that kind of life is to offer all of me for all of Him. The way Paul says it in Romans 8 is that we put to death the sinful nature and we allow the Holy Spirit to give us a new one, and that is Himself.

A friend of mine told me, "I can't even give Jesus all of me. He has to come and help me give Him all of me." She is right. That is how weak we are, and right now the enemy may be telling you with a little voice, "Oh, that is just Stephanie. That's for really spiritual Christians. That's not for me," and it's not true. The kind of life we are talking about—all of Him for all of me, death to that sinful nature—that is the life you and I were created to live. Just like a car was meant for gasoline—or electricity for these new cars—you and I were meant to live filled with His Holy Spirit so that we can know Him—so that there would be nothing to separate us from Him, nothing between Jesus and me.

Is there anything that is between you and Jesus today?

Helen Roseveare had been on the mission field for four years. In the process of working so hard for God with many patients, long hours, hard days, and more responsibility than she could keep up with, she was becoming irritable with staff members, nurses, and other doctors. She was losing it, and she knew she had to get away to be alone with God. An African pastor took her away for a while, and as he and his wife and Helen sat around the fire, she didn't have to explain herself. He knew exactly what was going on.

After reading Galatians 2:20, "My old self has been crucified with Christ. It is no longer I who live but Christ lives in me," the pastor talked with Helen and drew a capital I with his foot in the sand. He looked at her and said, "We can see so much Helen that we can't see Jesus. Will you ever cross out the I?" Then he dug his foot across the I to make a cross. She knew that was the problem—the deadly I. After that, she thought he was going off on a bit of a tangent when he said, "I've noticed you drink a lot of coffee. When someone brings it to you, you sit and hold it until it cools off. May I suggest that every time you do that, you say, "Not I, Jesus, but You."

What is Jesus saying to you? Do you need to cross out the I today and let Jesus take full control so that there is nothing between you and Him?

You will go back home to a world that is desperate. When we give Him full control, we no longer live out of our own self-effort, but out of His life. He gives us courage to do what we could never do on our own. He gives power over sin and temptation that we have never had—the power to live and love like never before. Is there anything separating you from God? Do you need to come and sit at the empty tomb and let the blood of Jesus wash over you? Is Jesus enough? You are invited to come offer your life—all of Him for all of you.

My old self has been crucified with Christ. It is no longer I who live, but Christ lives in me. So I live in this earthly body by trusting in the Son of God, who loved me and gave himself for me (Galatians 2:20).

Chapter 24

Good Hope Farm

Patsy Lewis

Then Jesus went with them to the olive grove called Gethsemane, and he said, "Sit here while I go over there to pray." He took Peter and Zebedee's two sons, James and John, and he became anguished and distressed. He told them, "My soul is crushed with grief to the point of death. Stay here and keep watch with me" (Matthew 26:36-38).

As we embrace the cross with confident hope, God leads us on journeys we never dreamed possible. Come to the Fire has spread through many ministries that have begun or expanded as a result of prayer and God's leadership in the lives of CTTF women.

On the way to the summer Come to the Fire council meeting prior to the 2011 conference, Rondy and her friend Yori stopped for a personal prayer retreat in Gethsemane, Kentucky. A few days before leaving for their retreat, Yori and her husband had attended a sex trafficking awareness meeting in Nashville which Rondy was unable to attend; therefore, as they traveled, Rondy wanted to hear all about the information Yori had gleaned.

Rondy's heart was broken with the stories Yori shared and was processing all this as she took the Gethsemane prayer path at the retreat center the next morning. She was greatly impacted as she walked past the statues of the sleeping disciples. Around the bend only a few steps away was the statue depicting the agonizing Jesus in the Garden of Gethsemane. Rondy grieved and travailed with the weeping Jesus as He began to birth a vision in her heart.

From Kentucky, Rondy and Yori traveled to Grove City, Ohio, for the on-site prayer and preparation meeting of the CTTF council and local volunteers, and Rondy poured out bits and pieces of what God was revealing to her. She continued to keep an open heart to God's direction pondering what she, one woman, could do if she awakened to join Him in his grief over the evils surrounding her city and world.

At the Friday night session in Grove City, Rondy shared her Gethsemane story using slides to help us visualize how Peter, James, and John were so close to the travailing Jesus, yet sleeping! Her passionate message revealed that she had been greatly touched by the insights God was revealing and the words He was whispering regarding His vision. She sensed God leading her to spearhead the development of a ministry to women and girls who have been commercially sexually exploited.

With the Rest Stop prayer theme that year fresh in her thoughts, soon Rondy began to gather a prayer and ministry team, formulate a mission statement, and draw up a business plan for Rest Stop Ministries. Her passion was to restore the lives of women who had been rescued from sex trafficking by opening a long term residential home. At the Friday evening session in Grove City at

CTTF 2014, Rondy again was the speaker and told the continuation of the story she had shared in 2011.

Today Rondy is the founder and director of Rest Stop, located on a beautiful twenty-five acres with two homes, fruit trees, a rippling brook that God has provided in Lebanon, Tennessee—a place taken from tragedy to triumph—Good Hope Farm. During their two-year residency at Good Hope Farm, the women will have every need taken care of: housing, food, clothing, medical, dental, vision, therapy, education, and job training, in order that they will be completely independent at the end of their stay and can take their rightful place in society.[1]

Because of Rondy's connection with CTTF ministry, she had seen the result of extreme prayer efforts. Many Come to the Fire women have been involved in supporting Rest Stop with prayer and action. The mission of Rest Stop Ministries is to comprehensively restore survivors and stop the oppression of human trafficking. Rest Stop exists to **Rest**ore Survivors—**Stop** Oppression. That's what God does when we enter His rest, wait upon Him for direction and follow His call, resting in Him. He restores lives!

In his kindness God called you to share in his eternal glory by means of Christ Jesus. So after you have suffered a little while, he will restore, support, and strengthen you, and he will place you on a firm foundation. All power to him forever! Amen (I Peter 5:10-11).

Chapter 25

Mesmerized by God's Love

Nona-Sue Mellish

For the Lord is the Spirit, and wherever the Spirit of the Lord is, there is freedom...And the Lord—who is Spirit—makes us more and more like him as we are changed into his glorious image (II Corinthians 3:17-18).

As a young child I wanted to know that I was going to heaven. I was about five years old the first time I went to the altar and asked Jesus to save me. From that time until the year 2000, my relationship with the Lord was always fragile. There was often this question: "Are you really sure you're going to spend eternity in heaven?" Too much of the time I felt condemned, hearing this voice saying: "You're not pleasing God, not doing enough for Him, and not spiritual enough. You don't read your Bible or pray enough." Therefore, in my youth, I paved a way to the altar promising each time that I would do better and try harder. As I matured, the numerous trips to the altar lessened, but the battle still raged within.

Once when I went out with some dear friends for dinner, the husband asked, "Well, what good things has the Lord done in your life this week?" I looked him in the eyes and said, "I am so spiritually dry." The dryness continued, until one morning in August as I was reading a devotional written by Max Lucado. I got to the end and there was a prayer. It said, "Lord, keep me amazed and mesmerized by what you've done for me." I began to weep and pray, "God, I'm hanging on by the tips of my fingernails. Oh, how I want to be amazed and mesmerized by You, but I don't even know where to begin. You are going to have to do it!"

This began an awesome journey of filling a journal with thanksgiving and praises. I became more and more aware of His presence. I asked the Lord what had kept me from living this victorious life that I was now experiencing. He revealed to me, "You finally admitted that you couldn't do it. You were so burned out when you told me that I, God, was going to have to do it in you. Dear Daughter, what beautiful words to My ears. You've always understood that salvation is a free gift, but you've struggled and struggled with the concept that the working out of your salvation is also a free gift. You must rely on Me. I'm not looking for your offerings and sacrifices. I gave the supreme sacrifice when I gave My Son. Accept My love! When you fail and falter, don't tell Me you'll try harder, you'll do better next time. Come to Me and receive My love. Yes, you will do good works, those that are birthed out of an intimacy with me, and you will do them out of love for Me."

What occurred on that August 2000 morning is even deeper and richer today, because it has been a continual journey of maturing in the truth that He alone is my very great reward!

In November 2009, I documented an understanding of this truth in a paragraph preceding an acrostic I wrote entitled "Beauty in the Anguish:"

"On September 25, 2008, my husband, Tim, was diagnosed with cancer. The awareness that God is always at work, even in a situation such as this, resulted in a heart cry arising in my soul: "Lord, don't let me miss You in the midst of the craziness of life!" God was and continues to be faithful—giving me eyes to see His ever-present workings. Even though Tim passed away on August 10, 2009, I can say I know there are miracles happening all around me. They are present in those situations where experiences converge and mesh in brilliant harmony. The paradox is these occurrences are overwhelmingly orchestrated, yet easily missed or dismissed. When I am aware of this detailed connectedness, I know I am deeply loved by a God who is involved in the activity of amalgamation on my behalf. No matter how out of control life may appear, God provides these step-by-step marvelous mergers, empowering my heart to praise Him as the Maker of Ah ha Moments; Breathtaking Occurrences; Coincidences—Not!!!; Divine Choreography and Divine Orchestrations; Everything, Everywhere Entwined; Encounters of the Divine Kind."

This paragraph contains prophetic words that I have frequently needed to revisit. Since, 2008, the circumstances of life have continued to be "crazy," but the day Tim was diagnosed, the Lord began making me keenly aware of the truth that His abundant love notes are written all over His Divine Orchestrations. All I need to do is be willing to have eyes audacious enough to recognize these connective patterns, because they point to His character that has and will continue to victoriously carry me through.

I was able to attend CTTF in October 2014. I rode in the van with a group of ladies from Oklahoma. Our van was turned into the "Glory Wagon" as we traveled home from CTTF on Sunday. We had a glorious time of preaching, praising, and singing! We could share volumes, but the attached A-Z that we composed encapsulates some of the "Glory" each of us experienced! We became a bit creative, so the attributes in italics were "travel" oriented since we journeyed just over 1,900 miles together!

Come to the Fire A-Z:

We came to the Fire and we encountered You, Jesus! Praise You:

Awesome Revelator, Artist of Our Lives, *Ascender*

Burden Bearer and Burden Lifter, Balm for Damaged Emotions, *Baggage Handler*

Calmer of Our Nerves, Conqueror of Our Fears, *Communicator*

Delight and Desire Giver, Drawer and Preparer of Each of Us

Emancipator, Encourager Along the *Highway of Holiness*

Friend that Sticks Closer than a Brother, Fulfiller of Our Quest, *Fire Igniter*

Guardian Angel, *GPS—Glorious Positioning System*

Helper, Healer

Inspiration, Inspirer, Intimate Lover, Illuminator

Jump Starter

Keeper of Our Hearts

Lover of Our Souls, Life Giver and Life Saver, Living Lyrics Sung Over Us

Maker, Motivator, Majestic, *Mountain Mover by Minimizing Problems*

New Life, New Beginning, Newness, Night Light for the Dark Nights of Our Souls
Omnipotent Friend
Presence, Passenger in Our Glory Van, Puzzle Fitter
Quencher of Our Thirst, Quieter by Your Love
Renewer, Reliable and Refreshing Rest Stop
Sustainer, Scenic View Designer
Transformer, Travel Guide, Tank Filler
Uplifter
Victory; Victorious, Glorious Lord
Winner, Wonder, Washer, Water Giver (Living Water), Willing, Worthy
X-ray Technician, eXtremely Patient Re-calculator (even to the slightest detail)
Yoke Sharer, You Are Enough!
Zest for Life

For a child is born to us, a son is given to us. The government will rest on his shoulders. And he will be called: Wonderful Counselor, Mighty God, Everlasting Father, Prince of Peace. His government and its peace will never end. He will rule with fairness and justice from the throne of his ancestor David for all eternity. The passionate commitment of the LORD of Heaven's Armies will make this happen! (Isaiah 9:6-7).

His Fire Continues to Spread

CTTF Attendees

Anointed

Come to the Fire was a life changing experience for me, especially the healing service. I was raised in a cult, and even though I left as soon as I was old enough twenty-five years ago, it has had a lasting effect on me. I have suffered from mental health issues and been plagued with multiple voices in my head for years. I have been hospitalized and tried many meds to get rid of them, to no avail. During the healing service, I went to the altar and asked to be healed of the voices and to be anointed by the Holy Spirit so that I may help others who have gone through similar experiences. That is all I was able to tell Stephanie before God used her to bring healing to me. I did not tell her about having body memories in my feet and other areas of my body due to punishment I received from the cult for not doing what they wanted me to do. When she anointed me, she specifically anointed those areas of my body. At that moment the pain left, and for the first time in years my head is quiet and at peace.

Comforted

Prior to going to the Come to the Fire conference in 2013, I suffered a major loss in my life when my twin sister died. I took care of her for one and a half years before she passed away. God sustained me through that time, but I was emotionally drained. All my strength had gone into caring for Pam; however, when I look back, I can see that God was already preparing the place where He would meet me. I have been to several women's conferences, but Come to the Fire has been the most life changing one for me. I felt God's presence throughout the entire conference. Through the messages from the speakers, God was gently drawing me to Himself.

One meaningful moment was when I received a Bible verse that was meant for me. It was specific to what I was going through in my life at the time. "I remain confident of this: I will see the goodness of the Lord in the land of the living. Wait for the LORD; be strong and take heart and wait for the Lord" (Psalm 27:13-14 NIV). God knew exactly what I needed to draw me closer to Him and to trust Him with every detail of my life. God's timing is so perfect. Beth Coppedge said: "We are the book the world reads," and I want my book to be the presence of Jesus Christ in me, the hope of glory.

As the days approached for the 2014 conference, I was anxiously anticipating what God had already set in place for me. Since the loss of my twin, I continued to be grief stricken. I could not shake the feeling that half of me was gone, and I felt like I was just going through the motions. I knew God was with me every step of the way, but I still kept trying to handle it all by myself. When I arrived at the conference, once again I felt the presence of the Lord. I sensed Him drawing me closer and closer to Him.

As the healing service approached, God prompted me to go forward for prayer. He placed me in the hands of Aletha. Time stood still as she prayed over me. Slowly and gently, I knew God was drawing me to Himself, and once I was totally surrendered to Him, I felt Him release that grief from my body. The heaviest weight had been lifted, and I experienced true joy. I can't praise Him enough. I finally felt that I truly could go forward with what He has planned for my life. Once again I received the perfect verse that was meant just for me: "...whatever we ask we receive from Him, because we keep His commandments and do the things that are pleasing in His sight" (1 John 3:22 NASB).

Simulcast Strengthened

In 2007, my sister from Texas invited me to attend the second Come to the Fire Conference. I flew from Arkansas and stayed in the hotel with her. She took care of all lodging, rental car, and transportation details back and forth from the conference. I have attended every conference since either in person or through simulcast. The doors closed for me to attend the live conference in 2013, so I live streamed it at my home, and more than twenty ladies attended.

A devotional by Aletha that really impacted me was entitled "The Real Work." I had sensed for a year the Holy Spirit leading me to live stream the conference at our church. I worried and even argued with God, anxious about results, who would come and who would be willing to work with me? While reading her Spirit-directed words from her personal testimony of leaving the results to God, He gave me peace and direction for what He had been asking of me.

I began preparing to hold the simulcast at my church and invited ladies from around the state to be on a planning committee. I prayerfully organized, as I had watched the CTTF team do in previous years, with ushers, greeters, prayer team participants, anointers for the healing service, and prayer gatherings leading up to the conference. The Holy Spirit prepared and opened the hearts of my pastor, local church members, our district leaders, and surrounding churches to say "yes" to participate in live streaming the conference. Within days, the Holy Spirit had the team in place; more than thirty people from multiple churches, Celebrate Recovery leadership, and our Men's Ministry personnel signed on to bring the Fire to Arkansas. The Spirit was faithful to remind our team that if God does the work, we cannot fail.

After months of prayer and planning, we were ready for God's Spirit to be outpoured as we participated in Arkansas with ladies from many states and nations who had gathered in Grove City, Ohio, for Come to the Fire. From throughout our state, hungry ladies with eager hearts came to the simulcast. At the end of the conference, I felt led to ask for testimonies, and many shared. We heard reports of those who were transformed, sanctified, revived, and healed spiritually and emotionally. New prayer partners formed. Ladies from different churches who served on the servants' teams started praying together for their husbands, who had not claimed faith in Jesus. The seed the Holy Spirit planted in 2014 for a hunger for more of Jesus continues; we stay connected through prayer in the body of Christ.

Chapter 26

Advance

Patsy Lewis

So, my dear brothers and sisters, be strong and immovable. Always work enthusiastically for the Lord, for you know that nothing you do for the Lord is ever useless (I Corinthians 14:58).

When I was contemplating writing a conclusion for this manuscript, God seemed to say the word to use is ADVANCE. I understand what this means; there will never be a conclusion to Come to the Fire! Women who have been set free will celebrate that freedom in Christ eternally because it is true: "When the Son sets you free, you are free, indeed!"[1]

The year 2005 was spent praying and planning for the first Come to the Fire in October 2006. A few weeks prior to my first Come to the Fire council prayer and planning meeting, the news was filled with reports of wild fires that were spreading across Oklahoma. Since our children and grandchildren were all living in Oklahoma, we stayed glued to the television watching these reports. It was emotional for me because I had been trapped on the freeway during one of those fires several years before. As I viewed the wind carrying embers that ignited new fires, my prayer became, "Holy Spirit, do Your work of cleansing and purifying our hearts, blowing over Your conference to ignite revival fires across our nation and beyond!" I could envision it happening!

Kim McLean had finished writing the theme song on the plane as she traveled to that council meeting which was held several months before the first conference in 2006. We sat speechless when Kim sang the last phrase and strummed the final chord—then we fell on our faces in praise and worship thanking God for the song He had produced through Kim. I sang portions of the song over and over that evening and as I traveled home the next day. Kim quickly made copies of the words for us to take with us. When I arrived home, even before I unpacked, I sat on the arm of my husband's chair and sang "Come to the Fire" to him as he followed along.

Instead of being speechless when we sang the final word, he jumped to his feet and exclaimed, "That's it! We're going to have Come to the Fire prayer days for pastors and leaders." Immediately we started planning days of prayer at various locations across our state. The fire was already spreading. Each morning I would light the fire in the fireplace and fall on my face asking God to prepare my heart for His holy visitation.[1] My prayers were united with thousands of others, and God answered by pouring out His Spirit at every conference.

Ten years later, after nine conferences, God called the council to a year of sabbatical in 2015. For several months, long before the Come to the Fire conference on October 2-4, 2014, I wondered if God might be leading us to take a sabbatical. If this was His leading, I knew He would confirm it with CTTF director Aletha Hinthorn and perhaps other council members.

I came home from the glorious CTTF conference in Grove City, and as I continued to ponder the thought of taking a sabbatical, I read all the accounts of Moses and the Israelites waiting and watching as a cloud hovered over the tabernacle—never journeying until the cloud moved—indicating God's presence and direction for them to follow.

The LORD went ahead of them. He guided them during the day with a pillar of cloud, and he provided light at night with a pillar of fire. This allowed them to travel by day or by night (Exodus 13:21).

Then the cloud covered the Tabernacle, and the glory of the LORD filled the Tabernacle. Moses could no longer enter the Tabernacle because the cloud had settled down over it, and the glory of the LORD filled the Tabernacle. Now whenever the cloud lifted from the Tabernacle, the people of Israel would set out on their journey, following it. But if the cloud did not rise, they remained where they were until it lifted. The cloud of the LORD hovered over the Tabernacle during the day, and at night, fire glowed inside the cloud so the whole family of Israel could see it. This continued throughout all their journeys (Exodus 40:34-38).[2]

I was wondering if we needed a year for renewal. I read Exodus 23:10-11. "Plant and harvest your crops for six years, but let the land be renewed and lie uncultivated during the seventh year."

I began to ask God to reveal any idols that we or attendees could be in danger of erecting. Following the 2009 conference, my daughter, Lanissa, suggested we needed a heavy prayer covering following the conference, and she compiled a list of ways for us to pray. We have used these guidelines for praying after every conference since. I had been fervently praying over two points she had suggested:

• That the altars that were built at CTTF would truly glorify God but not become our idols.

• That our boast be in Christ, not self, not a speaker, not a conference, not a singer, song, or book.

I was convinced that we needed a year of rest, seeking His face, and making our council meetings times of prayer. Numbers 9 repeatedly states, "At the LORD's command they encamped, and at the LORD's command they set out."

This was one journal entry as I listened for Gods's direction:

"The way will become clear. When the fire in the cloud moves, you follow. My glory will go ahead lighting the way. A glorious unfolding is in the waiting. Prayer is the work at this time."

We continued to pray, and Aletha wrote to the council:

"Next year will be our sabbatical—a time of seeking God and allowing Him to search our hearts. We don't want Come to the Fire to become our idol. This year will not be time wasted, but will accomplish more than if we moved ahead in our self-efforts. The guidance of the Holy Spirit to call a Sabbatical reminds me of His presence in the early days of forming Come to the Fire. Numbers 9:15-23 repeatedly says that the Israelites constantly followed the cloud: 'At the commandment of the LORD they rested in the tents, and at the commandment of the LORD they journeyed.' He is calling us to 'rest in Him.'

Later Aletha sent this message in her weekly Fire Seekers article: "Many of you are asking, 'Where will Come to the Fire be in 2015?' God has made His will clear and has confirmed it again and again. We are taking a sabbatical and not having a conference. We will still be maintaining the office, sending devotionals, having council meetings, and doing whatever God puts in our hands to do for Him. I read this wonderful definition of the Hebrew word for LORD: He is the One who freely influences and molds history according to His plans. With that blessed assurance, we go forward with confidence in Him. 'At the commandment of the LORD they rested in the tents, and at the commandment of the LORD they journeyed'" (Numbers 9:23 KJV).

The vision God has given Aletha for Come to the Fire is bigger than anything that yet has been accomplished. We must have clear direction from God to fulfill His calling for Come to the Fire which is far beyond anything we have experienced. Only He knows what that looks like. We must wait and hear what is on His heart and how He wants His purposes accomplished.

With every story I hear from Come to the Fire attendees, I realize God has answered my early prayer that His Holy Spirit would blow over Come to the Fire and carry the sparks and embers to ignite revival across our nation and beyond. That continues to be my prayer as we carry out His vision for Kingdom advancement. Lead on, O King Eternal! We follow, not one step ahead, but not lagging one step behind! At Your command, we advance!

Be on guard. Stand firm in the faith. Be courageous. Be strong. And do everything with love (I Corinthians 16:13-14).

Notes

Introduction

1. Patsy Lewis, *Come to the Fire Testimonies* (Come to the Fire, 2010) 13-18. [Portions of this chapter are revised and used by permission.]

Chapter 1

1. Patsy Lewis, *Come to the Fire Testimonies* (Leawood, Kansas: Come to the Fire, 2010) 135-141. [Portions of this chapter are revised and used by permission.]

Chapter 2

1. Patsy Lewis, *Come to the Fire Testimonies* (Come to the Fire, 2010) 79-82. [Chapter by Sharon Bushey used by permission.]
2. "Come to the Fire" theme song written by Kim McLean.
3. Ibid.
4. Ibid.
5. Read Rahab's story in Josh. 2, 6, and see Matt. 1:5.

I. Reflections

1. "Women Tell What Come to the Fire Meant to Them," *Women Alive*, January/February 2007, 16.
2. Ibid.
3. Ibid., 17.
4. Patsy Lewis, *Come to the Fire Testimonies* (Come to the Fire, 2010) 55-57.

Chapter 3

1. Taken from google.com, The Glory of God-God.net.
2. Gen. 1:3a, 12b, 30b, 31a.
3. Gen. 3:1-6.
4. Duet. 7:9-11.
5. Ex. 25:8.
6. Deut. 11:1-22.
7. Deut. 28:9-10.
8. Eph. 1:4; Gal. 1:4.
9. Jn.1:14.
10. Jn. 14:23; Eph. 3:16-17.
11. I Pet. 1:19-20 ; Rev. 13:8.

12. Eph. 1:11-14

13. 2 Cor. 2:16.

Chapter 4

Beth Fox, Mary Burchel, Patsy Lewis. "Worship at the Front Lines" Embrace the Cross, CD (Hip and Holy, a division of HCT Media, LLC, 2011), track 5. Used by permission.

Chapter 5

1. Patsy Lewis, *Come to the Fire Testimonies* (Come to the Fire, 2010) 41-44. [Portions of this chapter by Ani Simmons are revised and used by permission.]

2. I Cor. 2:14-16.

Chapter 6

1. Cheryl Roland is a Come to the Fire council member who has given her testimony at CTTF conferences and spoken for altar encouragers' meetings before the conference.

2. David Wilkerson, *At Wit's End*, (Internet search, World Challenge Pulpit Series, January 13, 2012)

3. John Henry Jowett, *Springs in the Desert*: Studies in the Psalms, (Baker Book House, Grand Rapids MI, 1976) 21.

4. Ibid.

5. Oswald Chambers, *My Utmost for His Highest* (Barbour and Company, Inc., 1963) 18.

6. Gal. 5:22-23.

7. Jam. 3:10

8. Oswald Chambers, *My Utmost for His Highest*, 40-41.

9. Elmer Towns, *The Beginner's Guide to Fasting*, (Regal Books, Gospel Light, 2001), 102.

10. Mal. 3:10.

11. Richard J. Foster, *Celebration of Discipline*, (Harper & Row, Publishers, San Francisco, 1988) 62-63.

III. Reflections

1. "Broken and Poured Out," *Come to the Fire* Magazine, November/December 2008, 7.

Chapter 7

1.   Patsy Lewis, *Come to the Fire Testimonies* (Come to the Fire, 2010) 19-26. [Portions of this chapter by Jan Wilson are revised and used by permission.]

2.   Rom. 8:31

Chapter 8

1.   Message presented by Linda Seaman Friday night at Come to the Fire 2009 in Nashville, Tennessee.

Chapter 10

1.   Patsy Lewis, *Come to the Fire Testimonies* (Come to the Fire, 2010) 112-114. [Portions of this chapter are revised and used by permission.]

Reflections V

1.   Patsy Lewis, *Come to the Fire Testimonies* (Come to the Fire, 2010) 117-118. [Portions are revised and used by permission.]

Chapter 11

1.   This message was presented by Cricket Albertson at Come to the Fire, 2011, in Grove City, Ohio. The theme that year was "Enter His Rest." It is our desire that children learn early in life to love Jesus with all their heart and to rest in His love and forgiveness.

2.   Patsy Lewis, *Come to the Fire Testimonies* (Come to the Fire, 2010) 68.

3.   Ibid, 68-69.

Reflections VI

1.   Patsy Lewis, *Come to the Fire Testimonies* (Come to the Fire, 2010) 98-99. [Portions are revised and used by permission.]

2.   Patsy Lewis, *Come to the Fire Testimonies* (Come to the Fire, 2010) 123-125. [Portions are revised and used by permission.]

Chapter 13

1.   This message was presented by Kim McLean at Come to the Fire, 2012, at Olivet Nazarene University.

2.   Ps. 51:17

3.   Isa. 42:3

4.   Acts 17:28

5.   Jn. 8:7

6.   Gal. 5:22-23

7.   Kim McLean, Patsy Lewis, and Renita Koehn "A Story of His Grace" Overflow with Love, CD (Hip and Holy, a division of HCT Media, LLC, 2011), track 2. Used by permission.

Chapter 14

1.   This message was presented by Nancy Jesudass at Come to the Fire, 2012, at Olivet Nazarene University.

2.   Heb. 5:7

3.   Lk. 22:46

4.   Jon. 3

5.   Isa. 44:3

6.   Matt. 28:20

Chapter 15

1.   This testimony was given by Darcy Dill, Come to the Fire Worship Team member, Friday morning, October 18, 2013, at Come to the Fire in Holland Michigan.

Chapter 16

1.   Num. 20:8

2.   Num. 20:10

3.   I Chron. 13:7, 9

4.   I Chron. 14:10a

5.   I Chron. 14:10b

6.   I Chron. 14:14-15 -

7.   Jude 1

8.   I Thess. 5:23-24

9.   Jude 2

10.   Jude 5

11.   Jude 7

12.   Jude 12

13.   Jude 13

14.   Jude 24-25

15.   I Chron. 15:14-15

16.   Jude 24-25

Chapter 18

1.   Rev. 3:20

Chapter 19

1. Jenny was invited from the Come to the Fire audience to read a published story—then she revealed that it was her story.

2. Patsy Lewis, *Simply Rejoicing* (Kansas City, Mo.: Beacon Hill Press, 2013), 143-144.

Chapter 20

1. Several years ago, Mark Smith received Jesus Christ when reading God's Word alone. Now Mark and his wife direct MyFreeBible.org. It provides thousands of free Bibles to men, women and children. To order your free Bible, go to MyFreeBible.org.

2. Name has been changed.

3. ibid.

Chapter 21

1. Dorinda Biggs, Patsy Lewis, and Jo Apple, "The Great I Am" Enter His Rest - CD (Hip and Holy, a division of HCT Media, LLC, 2011) track 2. [Used by permission.]

Chapter 22

1. This message was delivered by Sonia Samayoa on Friday Morning at Come to the Fire 2014 in Grove City, Ohio.

2. Patsy Lewis, *Simply Praying* (Kansas City, Mo., Beacon Hill Press, 2006), 17-19.

Chapter 23

1. Message by Stephanie Hogan Come to the Fire 2014 in Grove City, Ohio.

2. 2 Pet. 1:4

3. Eph. 3:19

Chapter 24

1. See online article in *Engage Magazine*, "From Tragedy to Triumph: Shelter Opens for Survivors of Human Trafficking" by Carol Anne Eby, July 17, 2015.

Chapter 25

1. A-Z written by Nona-Sue Mellish and her Travel Buddies, Gwen Howard, Marilyn Hunter, Donna Keesee, Kathy Powell, Liz Ramkissoon, and Linda Wright.

Advance

1. Patsy Lewis, *Come to the Fire Testimonies* (Come to the Fire, 2010) 13-14.

2. See also Ex. 33:7-11 and Num. 9:15-22.

www.ingramcontent.com/pod-product-compliance
Lightning Source LLC
Chambersburg PA
CBHW051822090426
42736CB00011B/1601